WESTERNNESS

Alan Williamson

Westernness

A Meditation

University of Virginia Press
Charlottesville and London

University of Virginia Press
© 2006 by the Rector and Visitors of the University of Virginia
All rights reserved
Printed in the United States of America on acid-free paper

First published 2006

9 8 7 6 5 4 3 2 1

LIBRARY OF CONGRESS CATALOGING-IN-PUBLICATION DATA

Williamson, Alan (Alan Bacher), 1944–

   Westernness : a meditation / Alan Williamson.

      p.   cm. — (Under the sign of nature)

   Includes bibliographical references and index.

   ISBN 0-8139-2511-8 (cloth : alk. paper)

   1. American literature—West (U.S.)—History and criticism. 2. West
(U.S.)—Intellectual life. 3. West (U.S.)—In literature. 4. Art, American—
West (U.S.) 5. West (U.S.)—In art. I. Title. II. Series.

   PS271.W55 2006

   810.9′978—dc22
                                    2005014981

For Gary Snyder with gratitude for his friendship

Contents

Acknowledgments

I feel lucky to have taught at the University of California at Davis during a time when, remote from other fashions in the humanities, it fostered certain distinct and unusual areas of inquiry. As I would not have written *Almost a Girl* without Davis's object-relations-oriented psychoanalytic feminists, I would probably not have written this book without Gary Snyder and the ecologically minded thinkers who gathered around him. I would like to thank Jack Hicks, Scott MacLean, David Robertson, and the late Louis Owens for encouragement, for steering me to the right sources, and in some cases for reading a chapter or two in manuscript. I am extremely grateful to Sean McDonnell for his help as my research assistant.

I want particularly to thank the University of California at Davis for a very generous Publication Assistance Grant, which enabled me to include full-color illustrations.

I also want to thank the people who have supported almost all of my work. Richard Wertime read every page of the manuscript and offered, as always, particularly useful criticism. My mother, Jehanne Williamson, and my daughter, Elizabeth Williamson, accompanied me on many of the "research" trips behind this book. So did Jeanne Foster, who also listened to almost all of the more personal sections read out loud. Naomi Schwartz encouraged me, from early on, both to take an interest in and to write about California painters. My editor at the University of Virginia Press, Cathie Brettschneider, played a decisive role, by being, from the start, as interested in the "creative nonfiction" dimension of this book as in the scholarly one.

*   *   *   *

The two "China Trade" chapters appeared, in a much earlier version, in the *American Poetry Review*, under the title "Western Voices"; reprinted by permission. "Some Tenses of Snyder" originally appeared in *Gary Snyder: Dimensions of a Life*, ed. Jon Halper (Sierra Club Books, 1991); "Thiebaud and the City" in *Jacaranda Review*.

"A Walk" by Gary Snyder, from *The Back Country*, copyright 1968 by Gary Snyder. Reprinted by permission of New Directions Publishing Corporation. "Hay for the Horses," copyright 1958 by Gary Snyder, is reprinted by Mr. Snyder's own permission. Quotations from *Mountains and Rivers Without End*, by Gary Snyder, copyright 1996 by Gary Snyder. Reprinted by permission of Counterpoint Press, a member of Perseus Books, LLC. Excerpts from *The Early Poems of Yvor Winters, 1920–1928*, edited by Alan Swallow, copyright 1966, and excerpts from *The Selected Poems of Yvor Winters*, edited by R. L. Barth, copyright 1999. Reprinted by permission of Swallow Press/Ohio University Press. *Roan Stallion*, copyright 1925, 1929 and renewed 1953, 1957 by Robinson Jeffers, "Apology for Bad Dreams," copyright 1925 and renewed 1953 Robinson Jeffers, "Contemplation of the Sword," copyright 1941 by Robinson Jeffers, "Rock and Hawk," copyright 1952 and renewed 1962 by Donnan Jeffers and Garth Jeffers, "Night," copyright 1925 and renewed 1953 by Robinson Jeffers, "The Purse Seine," copyright 1938 and renewed 1966 by Donnan Jeffers and Garth Jeffers, from *Selected Poetry of Robinson Jeffers* by Robinson Jeffers. Used by permission of Random House, Inc. Excerpts from "Tamar" from *The Collected Poetry of Robinson Jeffers*, edited by Tim Hunt, volume 1, 1920–1928, and excerpts from "Thurso's Landing" and "Blind Horses" from *The Collected Poetry of Robinson Jeffers*, edited by Tim Hunt, volume 2, 1928–1938, copyright by Jeffers Literary Properties. Used by permission of Stanford University Press. "Blackened Rings," copyright 1996 by Virginia Hamilton Adair, from *Ants on the Melon* by Virginia Hamilton Adair. Used by permission of Random House, Inc. Various excerpts from *Listening to the Candle* by Peter Dale Scott, copyright 1992 by Peter Dale Scott. Reprinted by permission of New Directions Publishing Corporation. Excerpts from "Book of Life," "California Plush," "Golden State," and "Self-Portrait 1969" from *In the Western Night: Collected Poems 1965–1990* by

Frank Bidart, copyright 1990 by Frank Bidart. Reprinted by permission of Farrar, Straus, and Giroux, LLC, and Carcanet Press, Ltd. Excerpts from *Four Good Things*, by James McMichael, reprinted by permission of James McMichael. Excerpts from *Given Sugar, Given Salt* by Jane Hirshfield, copyright 2001 by Jane Hirshfield. Reprinted by permission of HarperCollins Publishers, Inc. Excerpts from "A Foghorn" and "The Rat" in *Bright Existence* by Brenda Hillman, copyright 1993. Reprinted by permission of Wesleyan University Press. Excerpts from "My Mother's Nipples" from *Sun Under Wood* by Robert Hass, copyright 1996 by Robert Hass. Reprinted by permission of HarperCollins Publishers, Inc. Excerpts from "A Magic Mountain" and "The Separate Notebooks" from *The Collected Poems, 1931–1987* by Czeslaw Milosz, copyright 1988 by Czeslaw Milosz Royalties, Inc. Reprinted by permission of HarperCollins Publishers, Inc.

Prologue

I am a transplanted westerner but also, in some sense, a real one. My parents weren't born here, but they finished their growing-up here and always identified more with the West than the East. My father was never happier than on the early summer mornings when he pointed the family car away from Chicago, toward our summer home in Monterey. I too liked Monterey best as a small child, when nature and family were enough. Later, things changed. I was the kind of shy, awkward, unathletic kid who doesn't fare well in places like the public swimming pools of Monterey. So I was thrown back mainly on the company of my parents and grandparents—a situation no adolescent finds completely comfortable. The eternal fog that hugs the coastline in the summer months came to symbolize my being cut-off from whatever was most vivid in myself. Chicago, by contrast—where I went to a private high school, where I had first loves, where I invoked the dense-leaved, humid late springs in my first literary efforts—became my imprinted landscape. At last, I went East to college and found it, as the poet Frank Bidart wrote of his own eastward translation, "more like me / than I had let myself hope."[1]

In 1982, the exigencies of my career brought me back to live in California, only a two hours' drive from the scenes of my childhood summers. It was a renewed encounter with childhood wonder but also with childhood loneliness. I feared that the self I had made in my eastern years might dissolve into that miasma of muted feelings, muted powers I remembered so strongly from my late adolescent summers. In fact, moving West was a new beginning for me as a writer, but I wouldn't know that for some years to come.

Because of my background, I have a double relation to west-

ern literature. I read western writers—whether it's Cather, Steinbeck, or Snyder—with a feeling of returning to a dialect I've always known, that I can't not understand. I look at western paintings with the same feeling. Yet I retain enough of the outsider's
perspective that the boisterous self-praise with which western literature finds itself the healthiest, and most underrated, version
of American literature irritates me; or seems, quite simply, beside
the point.

This literary war of East and West is an old, if, from my point
of view, an unfortunate one. If there is, occasionally, real condescension toward the West on the part of eastern critics, the
more bristlingly defensive western writers have sometimes made
themselves a virtual thought-police for their own kind. As Carol
Muske-Dukes reminds us, as far back as 1932 the anthologist
Helen Hoyt castigated Ina Coolbrith and Edwin Markham, two of
the best-known California poets up to that point, for "writing
about things un-Californian."[2]

One particularly memorable skirmish in this war was Edmund Wilson's salvo, "The Boys in the Back Room," and William
Everson's riposte, *Archetype West*. Wilson all but suggests that
westerners are incapable of producing major literature. California, he says, suffers from "the remoteness from the East and the
farther remoteness from Europe"; while it "looks . . . out upon a
wider ocean toward an Orient with which as yet any cultural
communication is difficult."[3] Even the weather conspires to
deny western writers a "weight proportionate to the bulk of their
work." In their "great open-air amphitheater," they are burdened
with the absence not only of "an attentive audience" but of
"acoustics to heighten and clarify the speeches":

> The paisanos of Tortilla Flat also eat, love and die in a
> golden and boundless sunlight that never becomes charged
> with their energies; and the rhapsodies of William
> Saroyan, diffused in this non-vibrant air, pass without
> repercussions. Even the monstrous, the would-be elemen-
> tal, the would-be barbaric tragedies which Robinson
> Jeffers heaps up are all a little like amorphous cloud-
> dramas that eventually fade out to sea.[4]

Everson's reply—like Emerson and Whitman's manifestos in the founding moments of American literature—transvalues every negative into a positive. Western literature will embody a new democratic consciousness, a new religious vision inspired by nature. It will leave behind the overintellectual, over-refined forms of European-influenced literature, as it will leave behind the hierarchical class structure of European-influenced society. If western writers sometimes seem to have "intensity without structure," they are following—as de Tocqueville and Perry Miller, as well as Whitman, saw—"the secret quest . . . of democracy itself," "the impulse to reject completely the gospel of civilization."[5] Westerners, as "*term* of the westward migration" [Everson's italics] are in fact the most typical Americans, "at the center, rather than on the periphery, of the American experience" (4–5). They experience their "boundless sunlight" not as a sound-deadening void but as the locus of a "pantheism" that is "*the* characteristic American religious and aesthetic feeling" (7). They have access to an "archetype," a "strong preoccupation with apotheosis" that, according to Everson, confers a "positive, if unconscious, value" on "violence" (13). And Everson goes on to suggest, as a number of western writers have, that the East is *really* still British: "The East Coast provinces . . . did not begin as democracies; they began as colonies of European derivation, and to this day manifest a residual hierarchical disposition, however diffused by its American transplantation" (8). ("Hierarchical" is a coded word for Everson; he also applies it to the formalist literary values of the New Critics, themselves, for him, an inappropriate "transplantation" on American ground [14–15].)

But Wilson's warnings, I believe, are not that easily dismissed. His oddly poignant, poetic prose about the "strange sense of unreality" in California, "the empty sun and the incessant rains . . . the hypnotic rhythms of day and night that revolve with unblurred uniformity," calls back for me some of my own feelings in adolescence.[6] Moreover, that distinguished native Californian historian, Kevin Starr, seems partly to agree with Wilson's sense of a paralyzing cultural vacuum mixed with unhelpful self-promotion. Reflecting on the many suicides among San Francisco's turn-of-the-century "Bohemians," he concludes that even when they were "pessimis[ts]" it "was a sign of provincialism and lack of major talent." They were indeed, it seems, too remote from Europe, receiving its outmoded intellectual fashions after a peculiar time-lapse, "at a time when avant-garde America, in Chicago, in New York, in European exile, was renewing itself through connection with the forward thrust of Continental aesthetics."

> The record of so much devastation makes one wonder whether California was not to blame. As a provincial culture, eager to upgrade itself, it authenticated its artists too easily and they in turn fell into an exaggerated sense of their own importance. . . . As a region, California offered itself too easily as a self-justifying symbol of spacious identity.[7]

Darker still is Starr's account of Jack London's last novel, *The Little Lady of the Big House.* In it, London's stand-in, Dick Forrest, is a physical superman, an innovative scientific rancher, a philosopher and patron of the arts, "cultured, modern, and at the same time profoundly primitive." Yet he is also childless and an alcoholic; his wife contemplates leaving him for another man; he thinks often of suicide, and his wife ultimately does kill herself, as London himself may have done.[8]

I have found one of the most illuminating ways to think about western literature is that it perhaps repeats, at about seventy-five to a hundred years' distance, the trajectory of American literature itself, in its anxieties as well as its drive for self-affirmation. I'm thinking not only about the anxiety about the responses of more established cultures (as Joel Porte reminds us, Cooper began writing his romance-novels in the very year of the controversy over Sydney Smith's challenge, "In the four quarters of the globe, who reads an American book?").[9] More profound fears are recorded in the darker writers of the American Renaissance—Hawthorne, Poe, Melville. What is it like to live in the face of a huge, alien, unpeopled landscape, and its dangers? What kinds of community will develop there? Idyllic, or narrow-minded, repressive, terrified, as Hawthorne felt looking back at the Salem witch trials? (Poe's horror, William Carlos Williams wrote, was really the horror of a "world of unreality, a formless 'population'—drifting and feeding," and it was because he resisted, rather than catering to, "the contamination of the UNFORMED LUMP," that "in him American literature is anchored.")[10] And what, too, of the guilt of having taken the land away from its original inhabitants? Can it only be denied and forgotten, or is there some possibility, as Everson believed—following on such eastern writers as Hart Crane—of somehow inheriting something of the native outlook and so changing permanently white culture's religious consciousness, and consciousness of the land?

What, finally, about writing in such a context? Especially writing novels, which from their beginning have depended on elaborately structured societies, codes of manners, as background to the intricacy of individual characters? When Edmund Wilson complained that western literature merely declaimed to a "great open-air amphitheater," he echoed Hawthorne's and James's fear that we could not have novels without the greater weight of a longer past. Hawthorne spoke of how "actualities [are] so terribly insisted upon . . . in America . . . where there is no shadow, no antiquity, no mystery, no picturesque and gloomy wrong." James, writing about Hawthorne, expanded these no's to a page-long catalogue, "no ivied ruins" and even "no Epsom or Ascot."[11] (To which the great critic Randall Jarrell replied, "America is full of ruins, the ruins of hopes.")[12]

Western literature, like the literature of the early Republic, begins in a stammering mix of local-color tale, promotional pamphlet, stilted ode. In both cases, the first novels—whether one thinks of Cooper and Hawthorne, or London, or Cather, or the narrative poems of Robinson Jeffers—are romances, in which isolated protagonists suffer spiritual agons against a spare social background, remote in place or time. Painting, too, begins in an exaggeration of European Romanticism, then slowly comes to focus on the granular, the specific, the forbiddingly local. Nonce-forms are invented and prove curiously durable. Influences come to hand, amalgamating side traditions in the parent culture with much that is culturally remote. Maturity arrives, long before we have stopped stridently proclaiming it.

Western literature evolves, I would suggest, by confronting the same dark themes that preoccupied the writers of the American Renaissance. The loneliness of the landscape may, indeed, eventually be the vehicle for new visions; but on the way it will provoke many nightmares, and cause many deaths. The Native

American past may be wrestled into giving its blessing, by a D. H. Lawrence, or by Cather's Thea in *The Song of the Lark*; but its curse will be audible too, in works like Leslie Marmon Silko's *Ceremony*. Hawthorne's "terribl[e] insiste[nce]" of "actualities," of a self-decreed "daylight," will be felt in Cather's Moonstone or Santa Fe; at the same time that the failure of inherited moral structures will be acted out by a series of destructive anima figures, from Jeffers's Tamar to the "girl-dunnit" plot of the California thriller. And, all the while, the need to shape such experience literarily will produce both the awkwardnesses eastern critics can mock and the structures—not in any simple way "elemental," as Everson says (11), but homemade, quirky, efficient—that mark the beginnings of a new culture.

*   *   *   *

"God didn't go West. He died on the trail," says Harry Angstrom's sister, Mim—one of the more endearingly disreputable transplanted easterners in fiction—in John Updike's *Rabbit Is Rich*.[13] This seems both true and not true. The punitive, superego-ridden side of Jehovah, which is what Mim has in mind, still hovers over Robinson Jeffers's Carmel, as Christian symbology informs Bierstadt's paintings of Yosemite. But as we move on into the twentieth century, the West does seem to develop a syncretic sensibility of its own that is post-Christian without being merely secular. To quote Muske-Dukes again, "[l]iterary life at the western edge of the continent"—boosterism to the contrary—"has always been a curious combination of isolation and internationalism."[14] Anthropological curiosity about the native cultures only recently displaced looms large here. Science, too, is more prominent as a source of metaphor than in East Coast literature, and is less likely to be viewed as the enemy of poetic wonder. Perhaps this is a compensation for the relative paucity of "history"—in the sense of layered depths of Euro-American past—as a point of reference; more likely it simply speaks to the fact that nature, in its aspects of sheer power and surprise, simply bulks larger in western life than in eastern.

Finally, Edmund Wilson notwithstanding, there is no underestimating the importance of the access to the cultures of the Far East that finally became possible here. The Transcendentalists' intuition that a truly American religion would be closer to Buddhism or Hinduism than to the Judaeo-Christian tradition, carried West by spiritual pioneers like John Muir, met a culture already affected by Chinese and Japanese immigration. When Japanese spiritual informants actually crossed the Pacific—Nyogen Senzaki to his living-room zendo in Los Angeles, Shunryu Suzuki to the San Francisco Zen Center—California seemed the logical place to come. The translation work of Kenneth Rexroth and, later, Gary Snyder made Far Eastern literary conventions an option, whether taken up or not, for all subsequent West Coast poets. By now there are Caucasian Buddhists, I would hazard, in all fifty states, but most of them (at least in the Zen lineages) owe something either to Suzuki's tradition or, through Robert Aitken, to Senzaki's. The West in this sense begins to *be* the East; it is not just the terminus of the Euro-American myth of expansion, the "course of empire," but the gateway to a rounded world.

*   *   *   *

This book is not a systematic history, for which I entirely lack the competence. Mostly I have concentrated on the two landscapes, California and New Mexico, which were vivid to my imagination as a child. (Omissions, therefore, should not be considered in any way judgments; the fact that I write about only one Montana writer, who happened to be a colleague of my father's, does not mean that I am ignorant that there are others.)

My themes will be developed, not through the kind of detailed scholarly argument parts of this preface might suggest, but as a fugue of accumulating impressions. That is why I have called this book a "meditation." My hope is that it will have the virtues, as well as the limitations, of what Shunryu Suzuki Roshi called "beginner's mind"; and that it will tempt the reader back, all the more directly, to the poems, novels, and paintings themselves. The great French poet Saint-John Perse wrote, "criticism can cease to be parasitical by becoming a companionship, an 'anabasis' if you will, a return to the sea, the common sea from which the work itself was drawn, in its definitive, perhaps cruel, singularity."[15] That has always been my aspiration as a critic.

Cather and Romance

Several of Willa Cather's novels share a characteristic beginning. The camera pans in, almost from infinity, on some tiny spot in the American West. The feeling-tone is of utter lostness and desolation—human purpose seems so absent, so fragile.

> One January day, thirty years ago, the little town of
> Hanover, anchored on a windy Nebraska tableland, was
> trying not to be blown away. . . . The dwelling-houses
> were set about haphazard on the tough prairie sod; some
> of them looked as if they had been moved in overnight;
> and others as if they were straying off by themselves,
> headed straight for the open plain.

In the middle of this lostness, then, there is a character, often so vulnerable as to bear, for the audience, its whole brunt: in this case (from *O Pioneers!*), "On the sidewalk in front of one of the stores . . . a little Swede boy, crying bitterly. He was about five years old."[1]

Then, something happens. A tiny center of affection and attachment is established—a spark in the void, it seems, but it will open out until it fills the entire alien landscape with the richness of human emotion. A "little Bohemian girl" takes pity on the boy, lets him stroke her fur tippet, and shares with him the candy her uncle's cronies have given her. What we do not know—unless we are rereading—is that these two will be tragic lovers; they will end as they began, completely together in complete aloneness, shot dead by her husband in his orchard on the edge of the open fields.

In *The Song of the Lark*, the loneliness is less literal, more social, but equally acute. "Doctor Howard Archie had just come

up from a game of pool with the Jewish clothier and two travel-
ling men who happened to be staying overnight in Moonstone."
When he chooses to go back to his medical office, with its "worn,
unpainted floors" and isinglass stove, we hardly need to be told
that he has a "very unhappy marriage." He takes in the weird
beauty and luminousness of the midwinter night in the small
Colorado town set among gleaming white sand hills. But his
main thought is that "people were stupider than they need be; as
if on a night like this there ought to be something better to do
than to sleep nine hours." He wishes he were in Denver, hearing
Fay Templeton sing "See-Saw."[2] Yet his life, too, will find its center of warmth, in the Kronborg family and in his half-paternal,
half-erotic affection for the daughter Thea; and that affection, in
turn, will be the mainspring of Thea's extraordinary triumph, and
thus of the entire plot.

Perhaps the eeriest of all these parallel beginnings is that of
Death Comes for the Archbishop. For there, what terrifies is not
the landscape's size or loneliness, but its pathless uniformity, its
power of self-replication.

> The difficulty was that the country in which he found
> himself was so featureless—or rather, that it was crowded
> with features, all exactly alike. . . . One could not have
> believed that in the number of square miles a man is able
> to sweep with the eye there could be so many uniform red
> hills. He had been riding since early morning, and the look
> of the country had changed no more than if he had stood
> still.

The relatively small size of the hills ("flattened cones . . . the
shape of Mexican ovens") adds to the "geometrical nightmare."
So, too, does the fact that the smallest features of the landscape
repeat the pattern of the larger, like the fractals of chaos theory:
"And the junipers, too, were the shape of Mexican ovens. Every
conical hill was spotted with smaller cones of juniper, a uniform
yellowish green, as the hills were a uniform red."[3]

Here, too, there will eventually be a human recovery: the
Bishop's horse will scent water and lead him to a small, isolated
Mexican community that will seem to him an unfallen Eden. But
first there must be a recovery of the individuated, and the sym-

bolic. The Bishop notices "one juniper that differed in shape from the others." Its "two lateral, flat-lying branches, with a little crest of green in the centre, just above the cleavage . . . could not present more faithfully the form of the Cross" (18–19). Restored to a nature that has meaning, and a meaning familiar to his own tradition, the Bishop kneels and prays.

This seems to me one of the founding moments in western literature because it makes clear that what is sought is a relation *to* the landscape, not simply human relation *within* the landscape. But it also raises a persisting problem: can such relation come through pure attentiveness ("two lateral, flat-lying branches, with a little crest of green")? Or will it require the symbolic, and will the symbolic require the imposition of preexisting, alien structures of meaning?

*　　*　　*　　*

These openings, zeroing in out of nowhere (or *into* nowhere?) remind me a little of the tentative, dislocated, almost apologetic openings of some of the first authentically American works of fiction: "Four persons in all, two of each sex, they had managed to ascend a pile of trees, that had been uptorn by a tempest, to catch a view of the objects that surrounded them." "Half-way down a by-street of one of our New England towns stands a rusty wooden house." "Four individuals, in whose fortunes we should be glad to interest the reader, happened to be standing in one of the saloons of the sculpture gallery in the Capitol at Rome."[4] These early American writers—Cooper, Hawthorne, Melville—called their works not novels, but romances. What they meant by the term involved not merely fantastic or melodramatic events, such as might be appropriate to a half-explored frontier, but a different way of presenting reality. There was a certain paucity of social background and texture, an emphasis rather on the symbolic, that made for "abstraction and profundity."[5] As Richard Chase defines the distinction:

> The novel renders reality closely and in comprehensive
> detail. It takes a group of people and sets them going about
> the business of life. We come to see these people in their
> real complexity of temperament and motive. They are in

explicable relation to nature, to their social class, to each other, and to their own past. Character is more important than action or plot.

The romance, by contrast,

> feels free to render reality in less volume and detail. It tends to prefer action to character. . . . The characters . . . will not be complexly related to each other or to society or to the past. Human beings will on the whole be shown in ideal relation—that is, they will share emotions only after these have become abstract or symbolic. . . . In American romances it will not matter much what class people come from.[6]

This indifference to class, and to "a group of people . . . going about the business of life," stems plausibly from a sense that social life in America is too unfixed or, where it is fixed, rigid and monotonous. Cooper spoke of a "poverty of materials."[7] Hawthorne, as we have seen, half-ironically complained of the difficulties for a writer where there was "no shadow, no antiquity, no mystery" but only a "broad and simple daylight" where "actualities [are] terribly insisted upon."[8] (The complaint is ironic, of course, because Hawthorne's best subject was the darkness he found in American repressions.)

In place of social rendering, the romance turns to methods more characteristic of poetry than the novel. There are masses of lyric description; there are also emblematic events, often "astonishing," with a "symbolic or ideological, rather than a realistic, plausibility."[9]

Several of Willa Cather's novels seem to me to reinvent the lyrical and episodic methods of romance, three-quarters of a century later, in the face of a parallel loneliness and sense of impoverishment. None does so more than *Death Comes for the Archbishop.* Father Latour leaves the one society in which he is grounded, provincial France; the traditional societies of the Southwest—Hispanic and Indian—remain richly fascinating but fundamentally ungraspable. His one sustained relation, over the course of the entire book, is with his vicar, Father Vaillant. And it is, for all the warmth of rendering, somewhat of an "ideal relation." Its developments and tensions all spring from the contrast, evident at the beginning, between Father Vaillant's extroversion and single-minded piety and Father Latour's more aristocratic, aesthetic detachment. Indeed, Father Latour himself says at one point, "I do not see you as you really are, Joseph; I see you through my affection for you" (49). There is one other, potentially highly charged relationship, of protagonist and antagonist, between Father Latour and the unorthodox, native New Mexican Padre Martinez of Taos. Martinez's bull-like sexuality and his potential for violence are as fruitfully antithetical to Latour's victories of sublimation as his vision of an indigenous form of Catholicism is to Latour's insistence on the rule of Rome. But where a novelist might have made their rivalry the main action, drawn out over hundreds of pages, Cather confines it to a single chapter.

Instead, the book is organized episodically, in a series of largely self-contained, emblematic encounters with the otherness of the Southwest. "Astonishing" enough in Chase's terms—stories of violence and the uncanny—they also have, like the cruciform tree at the beginning, "a symbolic or ideological, rather than a realistic, plausibility." On "The Lonely Road to Mora," where a late-winter storm transforms everything, making even "the faces of the two priests . . . purple and spotted in that singular light," they have a narrow escape from the "degenerate murderer" Buck Scales, a type of moral anarchy who is described with a wealth of satanic metaphors, and who has killed his own children in "ways so horrible that [his wife] could not relate it" (64, 72). Later, the Bishop travels to "cloud set Acoma," the farthest of the pueblos, and hears the story of its last priest, Fray Baltazar, who became a "tyrant" and was thrown over the cliff by his own people after he unintentionally killed a servant boy.

In the most memorable episode of all, the Bishop, lost in another blinding storm with his Indian guide, Jacinto, takes refuge in a secret ceremonial cave, inhabited, it would seem, by two divinities. The more tangible is an underground river, "perhaps as deep as the foot of the mountain," "one of the oldest voices of the earth" (130). The other, smelled and sensed but never seen, may be the "enormous serpent" of local gossip (123). (The title of the section, "Snake Root," merges the two in one suggestive figure of dark, unknowable origins.)

All of these episodes make New Mexico a place of unfathomable depths, beyond the characters' comprehension, though not beyond "symbolic" relation to familiar archetypes, whether of evil or divinity. The episodic, or tableau, method itself reminds one of the romance tradition: of the dozens of digressions in *Moby Dick*, between its realistic beginning and its melodramatic, allegorical end; of the many episodes in *The Marble Faun* in which the characters' responses to Italian settings or works of art convey their inner dramas, for which Hawthorne has supplied only the sketchiest supporting plot.

Cather herself was well aware of her departure from the traditions of the novel in *Death Comes for the Archbishop* and attributed them to a "style of legend, which is absolutely the reverse of dramatic treatment," in her letter to the Catholic journal *The Commonweal*. This famous letter does not mention the romance tradition, citing rather saints' lives and "the Puvis de Chavannes frescoes of the life of Saint Genevieve."[10] But she does mention it in her essay "The Novel Demeublé" in very similar terms. "One of the very earliest American romances," *The Scarlet Letter*, becomes an alternative model for fiction precisely because no one "could be sent there for information regarding the manners and dress and interiors of Puritan society." Rather, as in her letter to *The Commonweal*, "the mood is the thing": "in the twilight melancholy of that book, in its consistent mood, one can scarcely see the actual surroundings of the people: one feels them, rather, in the dusk."[11]

Cather's novels, I would suggest, tend toward the romance model in exact proportion to how early and unsettled a stage of frontier life they deal with. *The Song of the Lark, A Lost Lady*, and *The Professor's House* are novels—though they have romance elements, like "Tom Outland's Story,"· and resonate with anxiety about the limitations of social life in America. *Shadows on the Rock*, like *Death Comes for the Archbishop*, is romance pure and simple. *My Ántonia* surely begins as romance—think of the great prose poem to the prairie; the terrifying emblematic episodes of the Russians and the wolves, the man who throws himself into the threshing machine. It modulates toward novelistic complexity of relations (as does *O Pioneers!*) as eastern Nebraska becomes a settled community.

*   *   *   *

Richard Chase makes a further, particularly intriguing observation about the romance-novel: that it does not resolve, or even try to resolve, political or ethical contradictions into a higher unity. American works take "their energy and their form . . . from the perception and acceptance not of unities but of radical disunities."[12] Some years ago, a friend to whom I recommended *Death Comes for the Archbishop* could only see its hero as an extremely unsympathetic character trying to impose his moralistic brand of Catholicism on the entire Southwest. (And, one might add, preferring American expansion to either Hispanic or Indian autonomy, out of the purest pragmatism: "The Church can do more than the Fort to make these poor Mexicans 'good Americans.' And it is for the people's good; there is no other way in which they can better their condition" [36].)

At the time, I must admit, this objection wounded me—my identification with the book was then entirely poetic—but on repeated readings I cannot feel the book either sustains or refutes it. For one thing, the Bishop himself is on both sides on the issue of multiple, equally valid cultures. Early in the book, he disagrees with Father Vaillant, who finds the scholarship that detects pagan or Moslem origins behind Catholic practices "belittling" (45). He makes concessions that reveal a certain respect for the local cultures: he does not try to suppress the Penitentes; he never reveals the secret of Jacinto's ceremonial cave, though the memory of it fills him with "repugnance" (133). He profoundly disapproves of the Americans' expulsion of the Navajos to Bosque Redondo. However, as in a number of other situations, he refuses to speak out publicly, saying that "in a Protestant country the one thing a Roman priest could not do was to interfere in matters of Government" (296). The Bishop remains in inner disunity with himself, though in action, his goal is as single-minded as Father Vaillant's, the propagation of the Faith.

Of course, Padre Martinez is there to articulate an opposing point of view: that New Mexico has evolved its own indigenous brand of Catholicism, right for the people and the landscape; that Roman interference is abstract and destructive. But, as we have seen, Cather does not allow this conflict to develop dramatically;

though she develops it powerfully through the imagistic world around Martinez, and simply through the force that episodes like "Snake Root" give to enduring indigenous traditions. Here again, we find irresolution where we might expect resolution. Padre Martinez's schism succeeds, during his lifetime, at least in Taos; if the Bishop "wins," it is merely by outliving his adversary. And if there is any reconciliation of the "radical disunities" in the book, it is only in the appropriately emblematic form of the Bishop's cathedral, a repetition of the best of Europe—"good Midi Romanesque of the plainest"—yet part of the landscape it is made from, "seem[ing] to start directly out of those rose-colored hills" (271–72).

But I think there is a reason many readers—including myself, at one point—have found these political or cultural issues largely irrelevant to their experience of the book. The true drama of *Death Comes for the Archbishop* is an internal drama—that of the Archbishop's coming, in spite of himself, to love America *because* it is chaotic and uncontained.

This happens gradually in the course of the novel. On the journey to Acoma, Father Latour again, as at the beginning of the book, experiences the landscape as a kind of uncreation, "as if, with all the materials for world-making assembled, the Creator had desisted, gone away and left everything on the point of being brought together, on the eve of being arranged into mountain, plain, plateau" (95). Even the landscape seems like a ruin, the remains of "an enormous city." Yet it is not the mere "nightmare" of the plain of red hills. Rather, "[t]he whole country seemed fluid to the eye" because "continually reformed and re-coloured by the cloud shadows," in an "ever-varying distribution of light" (96). Taking refuge from a sudden violent storm in a cleft of rock, but seeing the far-off mountains still sunlit, the Bishop thinks that "the first Creation morning might have looked like this, when the dry land was first drawn up out of the deep, and all was confusion" (99). "Confusion" notwithstanding, there is a sense of a uniquely privileged vision—to be present at the Creation itself, when the world still shines with the waters of the barely separated "deep." True, the Bishop must again confront the terrifying side of New World otherness, in the natives of Acoma themselves. At Mass in the "gaunt, grim, grey" church, they seem to him

"antediluvian creatures," "rock-turtles on their rock." They ar
as out of reach of the "sacrifice on Calvary" as of Europe's "glor
ous history of desire and dreams" (100, 103). The price of accep
ing America remains very high, in terms of the despair or empt
ness that is all a European can see in the relinquishment of
European ideals. Still, the balance has tilted considerably since
the beginning of the book.

The image of uncreation recurs later, but only to provide a
background against which the Bishop can see himself and his
friends—Kit Carson, the Mexican rancheros, the priests—as sharing a common uniqueness. As they listen together to that "for-
eign instrument," the banjo, the Bishop sees the player's "seesaw-
ing yellow hand" as "los[ing] all form and bec[oming] a mere whirl
of matter in motion, like a patch of sandstorm." (One notices how
often, in the book, blinding storms are the outward manifestation
of American chaos and otherness.) The music, however, also speaks
to Latour of "a kind of madness; the recklessness, the call of wild
countries which all these men had felt and followed in one way
or another." And, watching the listeners, he realizes that "each of
these men not only had a story, but had become his story" (182–
83). Not only their identities, but a unique kind of identity, seems
to have arisen from having entered into, and assimilated, the desolation of formlessness. These men have become creatures of
myth. And Latour senses that he himself, for good or bad, shares
their fate.

So the true crisis of the book is not the conflict with Padre
Martinez, but the Archbishop's decision to "become his story":
to die in New Mexico rather than return to France as he had
always planned. Going back for a preliminary visit, he finds he
sees the Old World now with American eyes. "There was too
much past, perhaps. . . . It seemed to him that the grey dawn
lasted so long here, the country was a long while in coming to
life" (274–75).

In New Mexico, by contrast, "he always awoke a young man."
"His first consciousness was a sense of the light dry wind blow-
ing in through the windows, with the fragrance of hot sun and
sage-brush and sweet clover; a wind that made one's body feel
light and one's heart cry 'To-day, to-day,' like a child's." "Beautiful surroundings, the society of learned men, the charm of noble

women, the graces of art" cannot compensate him for the loss of this (275). The emptiness that desolated him so deeply, for so long, has turned into a "necessary" freshness—the very precondition for experiencing the present moment, even in old age.

If this experience seems so deeply felt, it may be partly because it was Cather's own. She was not a native westerner. She was born in Virginia, and when her family moved her to Nebraska at age nine, she found the treeless, barely settled prairie near Red Cloud "an erasure of personality," "bare as a piece of sheet iron." But as she was left alone with the landscape her first year there—her parents having too much else to occupy them—"the country and I had it out together," and it "gripped me with a passion that I have never been able to shake."[13] Cather, like the Archbishop, was an unwilling westerner; yet the West became the arena of her "passion" and her life's work, as of his, the place where she forged a unique identity. Though, unlike him, she did not want to be buried there. All her life, on return visits, she was afraid to "drowse and to dream" out on the prairie, in case death should catch her unaware in that emptiness, where there was "no place to hide."[14] She is, in fact, buried in the verdant landscape of Jaffrey, New Hampshire, with Mount Monadnock a safe enclosing rim.

The true artist, Cather wrote of Sarah Orne Jewett, "fades away into the land and people of his heart, he dies of love only to be born again."[15] The Christian image—even if it is addressed, on the surface, to an ideal of artistic impersonality—surely speaks to Cather's own "passion" for the region where her own personality had first to be erased. It resonates with something deep in her own life-history, and in that of some of her most memorable characters—Dr. Archie, Father Latour. All die to their old selves—and receive nothing tangible in return—for the sake of a place, or a person, as yet raw and unformed. Yet all are "born again," as they live to see their love reflected back as an unimaginable richness of feeling, an incalculable inhabitation.

Yosemite Painters

There are three of them—three, at least, who continue to compel attention. They make up not quite three generations, mid- to late nineteenth century, beginning not long after the Gold Rush. (Bierstadt made four visits to Yosemite in the 1860s and 1870s; Hill painted there from 1871 until his death in 1908; Keith began visiting a little later in the 1870s.) Their work is well represented at the Oakland Museum, and the DeYoung; there is a special treasure trove of Keith at St. Mary's College. Taken together, they make a fascinating allegory of the journey of the Euro-American imagination into the western landscape; beginning, as Father Latour begins in *Death Comes for the Archbishop,* with the importation of old symbols, ending in surrender to, and interpenetration with, the truly other.

Albert Bierstadt, the first of these painters, is the most famous outside California. (When the Tate Gallery in London put together an exhibition titled The American Sublime, he was the only one included.) He clearly found the West a lush and lavish new Eden. It is hard to resist his light playing and tumbling between thunderheads, over snow-covered Yosemite domes and white, serrated Colorado ridges. In his *California Spring* at the DeYoung, the thick paint seems to tremble to be bright enough for its subject. The branches of the valley oaks, close up, are shooting snakes of glitter. The massive cumulonimbus, sidelit from a sun hidden behind a darker cloud, make a sky out of Tiepolo or Poussin. Amid the lush, thick grass, the lavender and orange wildflowers stand out like little neon bulbs. (Eastern critics, it is said, could not believe the light-effects of early California painters were realistic: they were too bright, too clear.)

But serious lovers of West Coast painting often get a little mpatient with Bierstadt after a while. His awe at the West, though infectious, was preconditioned by received ideas of the sublime, from his training in Düsseldorf and his early association with the Hudson River Valley school. Painting Yosemite, as David Robertson has observed, he felt free to rearrange the landmarks for greater dramatic effect. He also preferred the light of a rising or setting sun, which, coming straight down the "east-west oriented" valley, as we can see in *The Yosemite Valley*, creates an all-encompassing radiance, "everything . . . joined together into a single whole by sharing the golden tone of the light." Even his centering sun, in the haziness, seems "more of a bright glow than a distinct disc, and since its radiance illumines the entire scene . . . more like a presence than an object."[1] Landmarks as solid as El Capitan, seen here on the right, become almost diaphanous against this background radiance. ("They'd blow over in one of our fall winds," wrote an early wit, of Bierstadt's mountains.)[2]

Bierstadt's Yosemite, Robertson goes on to say, seems "both real and unreal, both itself and a symbol of something else." Robertson's most interesting pages go on to show how Bierstadt imports European ideas of the symbolic and the religious. Borrowing, for instance, the convention of a descending beam of light illuminating the central figure from traditional portraits of the saints, Bierstadt—like his Hudson River Valley master Cole— draws in, so Robertson argues, the implication that "nature is a kind of scripture," of which the paintings are "translations." Bierstadt's centering sun has similar overtones: it "spreads its heavenly light over the entire landscape, and by making us look directly into it Bierstadt is helping us 'see' this divine presence."[3] Bierstadt, in short, is the allegorist of a "natural supernaturalism," in M. H. Abrams's phrase, which he brings west with him out of European Romanticism and Emersonian Transcendentalism. Like his technique, it expects to be enlarged and intensified, but not changed, by what it encounters.

Thomas Hill, too, aims at the sublime; but there is a crucial difference, one that quite removes the element of religious allegory. Hill understands that the true grandeur of Yosemite is not dependent on particular light-effects but is, rather, "the valley itself, in all its height, width, and depth."[4] Like Cézanne, he is an essentially spatial artist, though impressionist enough in his col-

The Yosemite Valley, Albert Bierstadt, 1868
Courtesy of the Oakland Museum of California; gift of Marguerite Laird,
in memory of Mr. and Mrs. P. W. Laird

Yosemite Falls, Thomas Hill, n.d.

Courtesy of the Oakland Museum of California; bequest of
Dr. Cecil E. Nixon

Headwaters of the San Joaquin, William Keith, 1878
Courtesy of the Oakland Museum of California; bequest of Elizabeth Keith Pond

D. H. Lawrence milking his cow Susan at Kiowa
Ranch

Courtesy of the Harry Ransom Humanities Research Center,
University of Texas at Austin

Stump in Red Hills, 1940, Georgia O'Keeffe, oil on canvas, 30 x 24 in.
Courtesy of the Georgia O'Keeffe Museum; gift of the Stéphane Janssen Trust, in memory of R. Michael Johns

Reflection, Gottardo Piazzoni, 1904

Courtesy of the Oakland Museum of California; gift of the estate of Marjorie Eaton by exchange

Visitation, Charles Rollo Peters, n.d.

Urban Square, Wayne Thiebaud, 1980
Courtesy of the Oakland Museum of California; gift of Dr. and Mrs. James B.
Graeser. Art © Wayne Thiebaud/Licensed by VAGA, New York, NY

oring. It's easy to sympathize with Robertson's view that Hill is the painter "who most successfully kept himself balanced between seeing and vision" when one looks at a painting like the Oakland Museum's *Yosemite Falls*. The canvas is full of perfectly calculated spatial tensions: cliffs slant down from right to left, and as some faces visibly tilt backward, others seem by contrast almost to lean out over us. Tiny trees at the top measure the scale. And the painting is full of motion, to dramatize the three-dimensional relations. Clouds boil up over the summit; the waterfall drops in three stages, with varying degrees of turbulence, finally to come to rest—as contrast and mirror—in a Constable-like limpid pool. Moreover, Hill's light is real; its splendor, no longer shaped by the conventions of European or religious art, feels somewhat alien. The pink glare on his cliffs, done in long impressionist strokes, catches the blanking-out of summer midday. (We can see the impressionist in Hill, also, in his clouds: like his sky, they have bits of *green* in them.) Here, one feels, are the real qualities—scale, vastness, light, and an alien dryness, even though water is the central player—that make one gasp, slightly, at the landscapes of the West. One is relieved, even exalted, by the airiness and soaring—but a little scared, as well.

We enter a darker world, literally and metaphorically, with the third Yosemite painter, William Keith. Turning to his landscapes with a Hill, or a Bierstadt, fresh in one's eye, it's easy to be disappointed with his mottled grays, browns, and greens. But it would be a great mistake to conclude, as Robertson does, that Keith's palette is "monotonous" because he aims at a kind of photorealism, because "[t]he painters at Dusseldorf had already headed Keith in the direction of meticulous realism, and his friendship with Muir made him want to continue down this path," and that "[t]here is a sameness about Yosemite—blue sky, dark green foliage, gray rocks—which becomes monotonous if viewed in painting after painting."[5] The fact is, Keith is a great colorist, but what his colors record is a dun, ancient, shaggy texture in the Sierra soil and rocks, grim and forbidding to the newcomer. His boulders lie around randomly, where they happened to fall. Many of the trees are snags. Lichen striations appeal to Keith, and dull olive masses of foliage that blend at a distance with the dull grays and browns of hillsides. His mountain torrents are green and impenetrable as a fish's belly. Yet Keith's colors, looked at closely, are never as uniform or dull as they look from a distance: the gray tree-bark glows with a dark underfieriness.

When Keith presents mountains, they loom, with a mass and menace in their lack of detail that Hill's glitter, awe-inspiring though it is, cannot encompass. Keith likes to put ragged, snow-covered peaks in the far background, as in *Hetch Hetchy Side Canyon I* at the DeYoung, or the Oakland Museum's *Headwaters of the San Joaquin*. But their presence does not suggest aspiration, the Gothic vaulting buttress, the signature of the Creator. Rather, their sharp edges, the flat ghostly pallor Keith gives the snow-fields, make us feel how they intensify the landscape's inhuman-ity; how hard it would be for us to survive them. (Keith may, in fact, have painted some of these canvases at base camp while John Muir was struggling for his life on Mount Ritter.)

I'm suggesting, in short, that Keith was a metaphysical real-ist, the first painter to struggle, in the details of his palette, with what is random, rubbly, prehistoric, utterly beyond the human scale, in the landscapes of the West. When he says, as Robertson quotes, "What I wish to make clear is that there are certain things in nature not to be painted so as to make an *agreeable* whole" (italics mine), I suspect he is voicing an aesthetic choice, not sim-ply venting frustration or excusing his own failure. He is, in an odd sense, a hundred years ahead of his time in his wish to claim the viewer's attention for what is not "agreeable," to "paint," as Jorie Graham wrote of Jackson Pollock, "what is not beauty."[6]

It is greatly to John Muir's credit that he was Keith's friend. But, as a practitioner of the art of prose, he only rarely reaches his friend's level of pure, neutral attention, as he does in this sen-tence: "anything like a bare cable appearance is prevented by the small, tasseled branchlets that extend all around them." Too often, Muir seems back with Bierstadt, overlaying the landscape with abstractions and adjectives as the latter did with luminous paint. And his Emersonian imports carry, with the greater explic-itness of language, the same idealist metaphor that Robertson has charted, of nature as a new temple, ritual, or sacred book:

The sugar pine is as free from conventionalities as the
most picturesque oaks. No two are alike, and though they

toss out their immense arms in what might seem ext[r]a[va]-
gant gestures they never lose their expression of seren[e]
majesty. They are the priests of pines and seem ever t[o]
addressing the surrounding forest. The yellow pine is
found growing with them on warm hillsides, and the s[il]-
ver fir on cool northern slopes; but, noble as these are,
the sugar pine is easily king, and spreads his arms abov[e]
them in blessing while they rock and wave in sign of
recognition.[7]

But George Santayana said, in a famous lecture in Berkeley in
1911, that western nature was inspiring precisely because it did
not offer a "transcendental logic" or a "sign of any deliberate
morality seated in the world." Rather it spoke of something un-
containable, "the variety, the unspeakable variety, of possible
life": "Everything is measurable and conditioned, indefinitely repeated, yet, in repetition, twisted somewhat from its old form."[8]
It is in Keith's painting that one finds this mixture of maddening
repetition and the strangely "twisted." John Muir is still read with
respect by environmentalists; but his true stylistic legacy resides
in the travel brochure, as Bierstadt's is found in the tourist art
galleries of Carmel. Something either cooler—as in Cather, Yvor
Winters, Gary Snyder—or more muscular, as in Lawrence and Jeffers, would be needed to give verbal shape to Keith's grays and
browns, his scaling rock, to Santayana's indefinite repetition and
"unspeakable variety."

Two Convalescents

In the 1920s, two men—two writers—came to New Mexico, in large part because it was a good climate for consumptives. One recovered, changed his style, and lived to a ripe old age as a cranky professor, the most formidable rationalist and literary conservative of his generation. The other went home to Europe and died, having experienced in the Southwest one of the few sustained periods in his life in which equanimity prevailed over pain and rage. They never met, as far as I know. For both of them, the great alienness of the West was a formative experience of the spirit.

*   *   *   *

D. H. Lawrence's round-the-world pilgrimage in search of physical and spiritual health brought him to Taos in September 1922, on his thirty-seventh birthday. He and Frieda had been invited there by Mabel Dodge Luhan, a celebrated patroness of the arts who was married to a Taos Pueblo Indian. Lawrence was to help Mabel write an autobiographical novel; but within days the project—and Frieda's jealousy of it—had them all screaming at each other. Notwithstanding, Mabel eventually gave Frieda a ranch, in exchange for the manuscript of *Sons and Lovers*. Lawrence adored the place and renamed it twice, as "Kiowa" and "Lobo." Today it belongs to the University of New Mexico. Perched at 8,600 feet in the mountains above Arroyo Hondo—high enough to cause altitude sickness in some visitors—it is still uncannily recognizable from Lawrence's opening description in *St. Mawr:* "the two cabins inside the rickety fence, the rather broken corral beyond, and behind all, tall, blue balsam pines, the round hills, the solid uprise of the mountain flank."[1]

Lawrence's heroine Lou Witt, in *St. Mawr*, immediately
"a certain latent holiness in the very atmosphere" that tells
ironically in the same words it told Brigham Young—"*This i*
place." The prospect of living there, almost as a hermit, seen
open the possibility of right relation with the universe, of b
"save[d] . . . from cheapness," that has failed her both in Eng
and American society, and in heterosexual love (159). And one
would not be far wrong to think this was true for Lawrence himself. "I think New Mexico was the greatest experience from the
outside world that I have ever had," he wrote; "the moment I saw
the brilliant, proud morning shine high up over the deserts of
Santa Fe, something stood still in my soul."[2]

For Lawrence, the Southwest is a magic country that both fulfills and transcends all Euro-American notions of beauty in landscape. As he says in the essay "New Mexico" that I have just
quoted: "Only the tawny eagle could really sail out into the
splendor of it all. Leo Stein once wrote to me: It is the most aes-
thetically-satisfying landscape I know. To me it was much more
than that. It had a splendid silent terror, and a vast far-and-wide
magnificence which made it way beyond mere aesthetic appreci-
ation" (96).

Yet, Lawrence makes clear that the landscape would not have
this power if there were not an element not only of irreducible
savagery but of irreducible chaos. In its more sublime form, this
savagery is a welcome corrective to Christianity's effort to sub-
sume nature into the idealizing principle. The "little woman from
New England," the previous owner of the ranch in *St. Mawr*—
who brings to it, of course, the legacy of Transcendentalism as
well as Christianity—first finds that the landscape fulfills her ideal
of "absolute beauty" but later must acknowledge a dark underside to that beauty, which undermines her faith:

> A very tall elegant pine-tree just above her cabin took the
> lightning and stood tall and elegant as before, but with a
> white seam spiralling from its crest, all down its tall
> trunk, to earth. The perfect scar, white and long as light-
> ning itself. And every time she looked at it, she said to
> herself, in spite of herself: *There is no Almighty loving*
> *God. . . . What nonsense about Jesus and a God of Love,*

*in a place like this! This is more awful and more splen-
did. I like it better.* (147, 149–50)

But always, underneath, in the "underlying rat dirt," the
"prowling, intense aerial electricity all the summer after June,"
the "bleached, unburied bones," lurks something less easy to
"like . . . better," a "savagery" that "is half sordid," "[t]he vast and
unrelenting will of the swarming lower life, working for ever
against man's attempt at a higher life, a further created being"
(152–53). Yet without this element, it seems, the place could not
work the terrible, healing magic it does for Lou, and did for Lawrence himself.

These paradoxes go far back in Lawrence's thinking. The need
to free the sacred from its Judaeo-Christian associations with idealism, goodness, perfected mental consciousness, goes back at
least to *Sons and Lovers,* where Paul says to Miriam: "I reckon a
crow is religious when it sails across the sky. But it only does it
because it feels itself carried to where it's going, not because it
thinks it is being eternal. . . . I don't believe God knows such a lot
about himself. . . . God doesn't *know* things, he *is* things."[3] Even
pantheism, in its western form, did not appeal much to Lawrence
because it still imposed too great a distinction between "God"
and the "things" God inhabits. Earlier in *St. Mawr,* another character explains, pondering on the original meaning of the word
"Pan": "In those days you saw the thing, you never saw the God
in it: I mean in the tree or the fountain or the animal. If you ever
saw the God instead of the thing, you died" (54).

Eastern religions might have resolved this problem for Lawrence, but they only created another one, in their rejection of
individuation and the active principle. The Buddhist doctrine of
no-self—"denial of the soul"—particularly repelled Lawrence. In
Ceylon, where he stopped briefly on his way to New Mexico, he
wrote, "I don't believe in Buddha—hate him in fact—his rat-hole
temples and his rat-hole religion"; and even went on to say: "The
East is not for me . . . a glimpse into the world before the Flood. I
can't quite get back into history. The soft, moist, elephantine prehistoric has sort of swamped in over my known world—and on
one drifts."[4]

All of this, I think, helps to explain why the Native American religions—as well as the landscape that produced them—had such an impact on Lawrence. Lawrence wrote in "New Mexico": "I had no permanent feeling of religion till I came to New Mexico. . . . It is curious that one should get a sense of living religion from the Red Indians, having failed to get it from Hindus or Sicilian Catholics or Cinghalese" (97). First, Native American religion seemed to him to embody the "oldest religion" in the world, a religion of direct experience, prior to the "god-concept":

> All is god. But it is not the pantheism we are accustomed to, which expresses itself as "God is everywhere, God is in everything." In the oldest religion, everything was alive, not supernaturally but naturally alive. There were only deeper and deeper streams of life. . . . It was a vast and pure religion, without idols or images, even mental ones. . . . It is the religion which precedes the god-concept, and therefore greater and deeper than any god-religion. (98)

Second, the Native American experience seemed to have room for duality, and for individual striving. As far back at least as the dark period of the First World War and *Women in Love*, Lawrence had been preoccupied with the need for dualism, not of spirit and matter but of good and evil, benevolence and malevolence—the "river of darkness" opposing the "silver river of life." Lawrence even argued, in a letter at that time, that we must "acknowledge the passionate evil that is in us."[5]

When Mabel Dodge Luhan took Lawrence to the Snake Dance at the Hopi Mesas, he responded first with a flippant piece focussing on the tourist response. But Mabel challenged him on its inadequacy and goaded him into perhaps the most profoundly religious essay he ever wrote.

The Native American world, Lawrence says in "The Hopi Snake Dance," though "alive," is a world in which "[t]he law of isolation is heavy on every creature." It is, moreover, a world in process, everything "emerg[ing] separately" from "great interrelated potencies."[6] And these great potencies—like Lawrence's two rivers, like the place-spirit of Lou's ranch—are dualistic. "For the great dragons from which we draw our vitality are all the time willing and unwilling that we should have being. . . . In the core of the first of suns . . . lies poison bitter as a rattlesnake's" (71).

In this world in process, divinity itself does not yet exist fully: "So that gods are the outcome, not the origin." And human heroic striving is not only valued—as Lawrence feared it was not, in Christianity, Hinduism, or Buddhism—it *is* the creation of divinity: "And the best gods that have resulted, so far, are men. But gods frail as flowers; which have also the godliness of things that have won perfection out of the terrific dragon-clutch of the cosmos" (67).

So the paradigmatic religious act is one that both reveres and challenges the cosmic energy with which it seeks contact. The young racers described in "New Mexico" gather their "male energy" to "come, by sheer cumulative hurtling effort of the bodies of men, into contact with the great cosmic source of vitality which gives strength, power" (98). The snake-dancers confronting the poison "[i]n the core of the first of suns" must "both submit . . . and conquer." "Conquered by man who has overcome his fears, the snakes must go back into the earth with his messages of tenderness, of request, and of power. They go back as rays of love to the dark heart of the first of suns. But they go back also as arrows shot clean by man's sapience and courage, into the resistant, malevolent heart of the earth's oldest, stubborn core" (71).

The Hopi religion appeals to Lawrence so strongly because it can honor both the principles of oneness and separateness, aggression and reverence. Lawrence's objection to Eastern religions is that they ignore the home truths of evolution and the food chain; they sublimate the aggressive element completely out of their cosmic unities. And Western interpretations of Native American religion particularly disgust him when they try to assimilate it to this benevolent monism:

> "Oh, the Indians," I heard a woman say, "they believe
> we are all brothers, the snakes are the Indians' brothers,
> and the Indians are the snakes' brothers. The Indians
> would never hurt the snakes, they won't hurt any animal.
> So the snakes won't bite the Indians. They are all brothers,
> and none of them hurt anybody."
> This sounds very nice, only more Hindoo than Hopi.
> (66)

How accurately did Lawrence understand the Hopi religion? Our current literary politics inclines us to be dubious, a priori. But Christopher Sindt has shown, in an unpublished doctoral dissertation, how closely Lawrence's descriptions correspond with those of Leslie Marmon Silko and Hertha Wong, especially as regards the truth of isolation and the truth of interdependence.[7] And Lawrence's interest in the situation of Native peoples went beyond the merely touristic; his piece in the *New York Times* against the Bursum Bill, which would have allowed Mexican and Anglo squatters to expropriate Pueblo lands, may have contributed to its defeat.[8]

In any case, Lawrence's vision of the Native vision offered him a way of resolving contradictions that have a long and tormented history in his work. These conflicts have to do with his animistic empathy, on the one hand, and his belief in hierarchy on the other. If the rhetoric, in *St. Mawr*, of the landscape's "peculiar undertone of squalor," as a "swarming lower life, working for ever against man's attempt at a higher life, a further created being" (61–62), savors of social Darwinism, it is no wonder. "In the struggle for existence," Lawrence says in a later New Mexico essay, "Reflections on the Death of a Porcupine," "if an effort on the part of any one type or species can finally destroy the other species, then the destroyer is of a more vital cycle of existence than the one destroyed." He then goes on to this flagrantly politically incorrect passage:

> Life is more vivid in the dandelion than in the green
> fern, or than in a palm tree.
> Life is more vivid in a snake than in a butterfly.
> Life is more vivid in a wren than in an alligator.
> Life is more vivid in a cat than in an ostrich.
> Life is more vivid in the Mexican who drives the wagon,
> than in the two horses in the wagon.
> Life is more vivid in me, than in the Mexican who
> drives the wagon for me.[9]

One might argue that it is "me," D. H. Lawrence, who is "more vivid" than the Mexican, not Anglo civilization generally, which he clearly sees as headed for the evolutionary trash heap. Still, one

nders what made Lawrence so intent on praising individual-
c striving, aggression, and hierarchies of superiority that it
ught him to the edge of a Eurocentrism he elsewhere despises.
e answer, I believe, lies in a conflation of metaphysical issues
h psychosexual and gender ones that goes far back in his writing, and in his personal history.

It is no accident, I would argue, that the East and Buddhist passivity call up in Lawrence the same rhetoric of inchoacy, of a "soft,
moist, elephantine prehistoric" that has "swamped in over my
known world," that, in *Women in Love,* Birkin associates with
the "sea-born Aphrodite" and the dominance of women over
men.[10] For the issues of separation and merging, peaceableness
and aggression, are always gender issues for Lawrence, as well as
religious ones. The rhetoric of "man, the farthest adventurer from
the dark heart of the first of suns, into the cosmos of creation,"
in "The Hopi Snake Dance" (71) echoes the praise in *Fantasia of
the Unconscious* of "Man, the doer, the knower." And the distrust of "oneness" as a principle by itself, there and in "Reflections," mirrors *Fantasia*'s fear that "woman, the great Mother,
who bore us from the womb of love"—and who, we might add,
therefore sides with the tender emotions, empathy, the "ideal"—
"is . . . the supreme Goddess."[11]

Indeed, *Fantasia*'s psycho-physiological system makes this
division the very basis of human nature as well as gender-iden-
tity. The sympathetic nervous system, where human consciousness begins, feels that "All is one with me. It is the one identity."
From this nervous system, we "rejoic[e] in the mother," and
"dra[w] love for the soul" (35–36). At the more developed level,
we even feel that "The other being is now the great positive reality, I myself am as nothing" (38). But in the "volitional" nervous
system, springing from the "lumbar ganglion," "I know that I am
I, in distinction from the whole universe, which is not as I am."
"From this centre" the child "kicks with glee," and "claws the
breast with a savage little rapacity" (35–36). And, Lawrence tells
us, "in . . . the 'natural' mode, man has his positivity in the volitional centres, and woman in the sympathetic" (97).

In short, for Lawrence, who, as I have argued elsewhere, fought
all his life against the strength of his maternal identification, to
affirm "volitional" separateness is to hold onto his very man-

hood.[12] If Christian love was annihilation to him, animist or pantheist visitation was painfully both a threat and a resource, as is evident in *Women in Love.* The Hopi offered Lawrence the middle way, which, in *Fantasia,* he had tried to locate in the very first division of cells. The Indian could remain male, finding his "positivity in the volitional centres," while yet reexperiencing the first insight, that "It is the one identity."

I hope it won't seem to trivialize Lawrence's religious thought to associate it with his gender anxieties. After all, the relation between the individuation principle and the problem of evil has been a difficult area for all religions, whether they optimistically invoke individuation as an "inner light," or whether they speak of delusion, karma, the personal devil. The paradox "Samsara is Nirvana" is the best that the most sophisticated Buddhist philosophy has done with the problem.

It is the same paradox, I think, that Lawrence finally approaches in "Reflections on the Death of a Porcupine." Conflict and hierarchy, he says, pertain only to the realm of "existence." There is another realm, called "being" or "the fourth dimension," where any creature—even the dandelion—"that attains to . . . its own *living* self, becomes unique, a nonpareil"; and "there it is perfect, it is beyond comparison." Moreover, to make things still more complicated, "The force which we call *vitality,* and which is the determining factor in the struggle for existence, is, however, derived also from the fourth dimension," that "region . . . where the dandelion blooms, and which men have called heaven" (88). The Hopi Snake Dance, where men revere the snakes by conquering them—but must risk being conquered themselves— could be seen as a sacrament revealing this mystery, the union of the comparable and the incomparable, "existence" and "being."

Lawrence's southwestern stay lasted, with interruptions, three years—making it, relatively, the longest period of stability after his departure from England at the end of the First World War. Though there are some memorable stories of his fits of rage there—as at every stage of his life, after his illness took hold—he looks remarkably serene in the famous pictures of him milking his cow and playing with the cat, Timsy Wemyss. In terms of his literary canon, New Mexico falls between the period of the "leadership novels"—which many readers find rather ugly in their anger at women, their fantasies of quasi-fascistic ruling male brotherhoods—and the period of "The Man Who Died" and *Lady Chatterley's Lover*, where he returns to imagining a perfect, monogamous love outside civilization. It was a bitter blow to Lawrence that he was never allowed to return to New Mexico, his tuberculosis being too advanced, by the late 1920s, to be concealed from American Immigration. But surely his withdrawal into landscape there—like that of his heroine, Lou, into celibacy—and subsequent clarification of his own religious vision prepared the way for his return to human generosity. In any case, no other prose, except Cather's, captures the experience of the overwhelming western landscape as freshness and invitation, as his does:

> [S]he could watch the vast, eagle-like wheeling of the daylight, that turned as the eagles which lived in the near rocks turned overhead in the blue, turning their luminous, dark-edged-patterned bellies upon the pure air, like winged orbs. So the daylight made the vast turn upon the desert, brushing the farthest outwatching mountains. And sometimes the vast strand of the desert would float with curious undulations and exhalations amid the blue fragility of mountains, whose upper edges were harder than the floating bases. (*St. Mawr*, 147)

*   *   *   *

Yvor Winters came to New Mexico, interrupting his studies at the University of Chicago, while he was still in his teens. He had discovered he had tuberculosis, and his family sent him to Sunmount Sanatorium near Santa Fe. He was a most precocious adolescent. He subscribed to *Poetry*, the *Little Review*, and *Others* from the sanatorium. He was beginning to learn French and to read the symbolists who had shaped the high modernists; and he read what was available on Native American poetry. (Only the earlier centuries of English literature, which would have so great an impact later, were unknown to him.)

After his release from the sanatorium, because of a temporary quarrel with his parents, Winters was obliged to earn his living teaching school in the mining towns of Madrid (pronounced, as Winters notes, *Mad*-rid) and Cerrillos, southeast of Santa Fe. Here is his wry, terse account of life in those towns:

Accidents, many fatal, were common in the mines, from which union organizers were vigorously excluded and sometimes removed; drunken violence was a daily and nightly occurrence in both towns; mayhem and murder were discussed with amusement. Yet I was treated with deference: I was able to keep order at the public dances on Friday nights merely by my presence until ten o'clock, but after ten, because of the consumption of liquor, I needed (and received) the assistance of the marshal. The miners tipped their hats to me when they passed me in the street; the Mexicans addressed me as Maestro, the others as Professor.[13]

In Madrid, Winters wrote several short books of poems, influenced by Stevens and Williams, which he later repudiated, but which for me have a freshness lacking in his later work. For a while, it even looked as if he might have gone a way comparable to Lawrence's. He was drawn to the sheer momentariness of Native American poetry, and to "'hindoo' theories of art" as "merging subject and object."[14] In his sequence of one-line poems, *The Magpie's Shadow*, one sometimes feels that momentariness carried the release, the fusion of self and world, that it does for the Japanese haiku masters:

> *May*
> Oh, evening in my hair!

> *Cool Nights*
> At night bare feet on flowers!

Coyote, the Native American trickster figure, seems, in "The Pines Are Shadows," to embody an electric transformativeness, an ungraspable, inexhaustible vitality, in the landscape:

> You have seen Coyote
> Who flows like gold,
> The runner in the night
> With eartips like the air.

But this poem is written as a dialogue, and its other character, the "Black Puppet" who opposes the "White Puppet," can only respond, "My passion is untold." And a much darker strain quickly enters into Winters's representations of New Mexico. More often, the poems envisage transformation as terribly neutral process, an entropy grinding up everything, in which the appeal of particulars counts for nothing at all. In "The Upper Meadows," the "hunter" may be "deep in summer," but he encounters

> Grass laid low by what comes,
> Feet or air—
> But motion, aging.

The landscape often seems peculiarly out of reach, "imperturbable," "impenetrable," as if a "cold of glass" had descended between it and the speaker:

> A pale horse,
> Mane of flowery dust,
> Runs too far
> For a sound
> To cross the river.   ("Jose's Country")

Often, the inanimate seems to have a power to reabsorb the animate into itself. The "dust" here, though "flowery," seems the substance, the horse the accident. Burros are "Like iron-filings / Gathered to / The adamant" ("The Solitude of Glass"); "Goatherds" are "inevitable as stones / And rare / As stones observed" ("Hill Burial"). The pace of things seems terribly, depressively slowed, even in the spring that "penetrated / Slowly / To the doorstep / Where the snow / Lay in gray patches" ("The Resurrection"). The train, once a "guardian" who "Strides through distance upon distance," now seems "Blind as a thread of water / Stirring through a cold like dust" ("The Moonlight"). There are constant reminders of death, and how it returns us, unequivocally, to the material world:

> Leal was dead.
> And still his wife
> Carried in pinelogs
> Split and yellow like a man's hair—
> Wet earth, shadow of the winter,
> Motionless beside the door.   ("The Resurrection")

Even the intensity of the erotic love poems—and some of them *are* intense—cannot quite dispel the knowledge that "night / stood irondomed / above the floor" ("The Lamplight"). Thought itself seems a defense against, or a momentary escape from, these realities, not a force that could turn them around and show them from a different angle. In one poignant moment, Winters confesses:

And it was not that
I did not believe in
God, but that the quiet
of the room was more
immediate—

    it was the
brute passivity
of rough dark wood   ("Midnight Wind")

The sheer otherness, coldness, inertia of the material world defeats the idea of God, without need for further proofs.

It's a short step, really, from this to the cantankerous older critic who would write, of Hart Crane's "The Dance," "one does not deal adequately with the subject of death and immortality by calling the soil Pocahontas, and by then writing a love poem to an imaginary maiden who bears the name Pocahontas."[15] It is an appallingly cranky misjudgment of a poem dense with both homo- and heterosexual Eros, and with an experience of intersubjectivity with nature, from the "laughing chains the water wove and threw" to the "padded foot / Within" the thunderhead, which Native American poetry, or Lawrence, would find quite congenial.[16] But if Winters had written the poem, it would have been an argument, and exactly the argument he says. Robert Hass writes trenchantly of Winters on the edge of his great rationalist "conversion":

He had . . . taken the imagist poem to one of its limits;
and, an American with Calvinist roots, he found the world
that he rendered, the world that was not an idea of the
world or an interpretation of the world or the world as a
mysterious symbol of something other than itself, insup-
portable. . . . In the desert he had discovered that the black

puppet was right. There is the world, and there is man; and man should not confuse himself with the world, because he is going to die.[17]

Winters's last free-verse poems on this theme, written in Moscow, Idaho, have a tone, as Hass rightly says, of "hysteria." Then comes Stanford, and a few coldly brilliant summary poems in form—"The Realization," "The Castle of Thorns." Then the slow deliquescence into a walking archaism, writing Ben Jonson poems in the mid-twentieth century.

It is tempting to blame Madrid for all of this. It's an Anglo town, of wood, tin, and shingles. When it goes it tilts crazily, at angles dictated by wind and dry rot. It's in the part of New Mexico Cather describes, the conical low hills echoed in conical juniper trees, with little other vegetation. Its particular topography, at the end of a long narrow valley framed by such hills, Winters aptly described as a "shark's mouth." In the '30s it was the site of a bloody last-ditch battle of mine owners against union organizers. Even in its prettified "ghost town" state, with craft galleries and an authentic drugstore soda fountain, a depression lurks, sadder and deeper than the squalor in Mexican towns. Simply to live there, one feels, rather than under the springing sun of Taos, might incline one to that northern metaphysics in which, where the human mind, the *Cogito*, ends, waste and trash begin.

Winters's prose poems show how sensitive he was to the economic sadness of the place. "The shacks were dull blue, gray, and brown, and most of them had been there for forty years. Back of the main street their arrangement was indefinite" ("Eternity"). He was sensitive, too, to the sadness of isolated men, afraid of their own and each other's violence. In "the hotels with sagging floors and long papery lace curtains swaying in the dark . . . I have always been unutterably sorry for the men I have passed in the corridors, yet I have seldom spoken to them—perhaps because when two men pass each other in a corridor a few hours before dawn, they look straight ahead as if they had seen no one" ("The Passing Night").

But of course, neither the look of the place, nor its economics, is a real explanation. We bring ourselves to landscapes—we don't just suffer them passively. Death was no academic topic to

Winters in Madrid; he and his fiancée, Janet Lewis, had bot[h]
a near brush with it in the sanatorium. And there are two un[char]
acteristically confessional lines in *The Bare Hills*—"My mot[her]
Foresaw deaths"—which, according to Thomas Parkinson, te[ll]
less than the literal truth. "His mother correctly predicted [the]
deaths of some twenty people, and when he was very yo[ung]
dragged him off to seances; his reaction drove him to his youthful interest in the sciences."[18] Perhaps the supernatural, or uncontained fantasy, was the one thing that finally scared him more
than annihilation itself.

> It was the dumb decision of the
> madness of my youth that left me with
> this cold eye for the fact   ("The Rows of Cold Trees")

Winters wrote these lines in one of the "hysterical" poems from
Moscow, Idaho. One believes that the West brought him near to
"madness" (or at least clinical depression), then to a "dumb decision" in favor of rationalism, by that same resistance to the human that, for Lawrence, was a liberation from suffocatingly close
bonds, allowing a large enough horizon for "man the last adventurer." Both men were spiritual, as well as physical, convalescents in the Southwest. Whichever we consider to have recovered, which to have succumbed, both left indelible portraits of
New Mexico's message to the Euro-American soul, if, as William
Blake said, "Everything possible to be believed is an image of
truth."

Las Trampas, Chimayo, the Georgia O'Keeffe Museum

If you take the back road from Taos to Santa Fe, through gentle mountains, sharp-pointed conifers that look briefly more like Colorado than New Mexico, you will come on two of the most extraordinary small churches in the Southwest. Both belong to the old Spanish culture of New Mexico and were built by the people themselves, not by missionaries or the church hierarchy. Las Trampas is sometimes called the Church of the Twelve Apostles, in honor of the twelve original settlers who worked on it. It dates from 1760 and is, as even the postcards will tell you, "one of the finest examples of Spanish colonial architecture." Chimayo is nineteenth-century, well on into the peculiar chthonic folk-Catholicism championed by Padre Martinez in *Death Comes for the Archbishop.*

One winds out of the forest into clear grazing land, and there is Las Trampas on its hilltop, giving a center to a hamlet otherwise too scattered to be called a town. At the top of its heavy adobe towers are wooden belfries like little birdcages, surmounted by miniature steeples, surmounted by the Cross. Why is it one of the most beautiful churches in the world to me, even though I have seen Chartres, the Duomo at Milan, Roncival? They are made out of the earth's solidity, its potential to uphold enormous leaps into the superhuman. Las Trampas is made of the earth's fragility, its power somehow to hold together against time and the odds. Everything seems dried-out and worn, allowed to be worn, and at the same time exquisitely cared for, whether by human hands or the dryness of the air itself. Everything seems, also, a little off balance, adding to the handmade feeling. The floor planks pitch at sea angles. A little panel, portraying a dove, tilts out over the altarpiece below, literalizing the image of descent from another dimension. Uneven corbels, at different slants, hold up the flat beam ceiling. Old wood, that fossilized gray.

This image of floating, of other dimensions, somehow dominates my impressions of the church. On a panel to the right of the altar, St. Francis seems suspended in air in front of a cross, denoting the stigmata. In the Transfiguration, above a side altar, Jesus, Moses, and Elijah, with triangular haloes, perch uneasily on a dark blue globe too small to hold all three. Above them a hawk-like dove descends; below, a saint prays in a turquoise nimbus backed by deeper green. The colors of the church generally, aside from the austere whitewash, tend toward blue and sea-green, not the bloodier reds you will see at Chimayo.

The handmade feeling, too, persists throughout. The chancel arch, sculpted in intricate wave- or cloud-shapes, is bare wood on the underside, incised with long slits. (Or is it perhaps a kind of plywood?) The Virgin is a little doll, all in white, with bridal veils.

Las Trampas looks most dramatic, on its hilltop, on a summer afternoon, with the white, swift outriders of an approaching thunderstorm behind it. Chimayo, by contrast, is sunk in a valley, its rounded submissive forms echoing the hills behind it. Its clay is a warmer, deeper beige. It has, even, a slightly gimcrack look, as if it were half a church, half a barn, because there is what appears to be a wooden shed, or attic, on top of the nave, with a corrugated iron roof. A ladder reaches up from below to a bare wooden door.

Here we are deep in a folk culture of magic and healing. Chimayo is literally a "santuario," not a church, and was only officially given to the Catholic Church in the 1920s, with the help of the writer Mary Austin. It is a pilgrimage site—at Holy Week, but really all the time. Old people with walkers approach the altar reverently and run their hands over the images of the saints. A man once carried a six-foot wooden cross all the way from Grants, 137 miles away, to offer it in gratitude that his son had returned safely from Vietnam. The cross is still on display.

But the true holy of holies is not in the main nave, but in two little rooms to one side. The walls, and even the rafters, of the first are hung with crutches, left behind in testimony by those who have been cured. A very low arched door leads to the farther room. Its floor is bare earth. In the center is a well-like circular hole, about a foot and a half across and about six inches deep. People kneel around it, reaching down inside, for it contains the sacred mud, which has the healing powers. The mud was known to the Indians for centuries; but, not surprisingly, there are a number of legends giving it a Hispanic, and a Christian, origin. Most involve the discovery of a miraculous cross, indicating the location of the special earth. It doesn't look particularly special, down in its pit, but it has a soft, attractive quality. While I was there I saw a little girl trail her fingers delicately, curiously across its surface, which held the imprint perfectly.

Chimayo seems to belong to the body, pain, and the earth, where Las Trampas belongs to the spirit. The Penitente cult is never far in the background in this part of New Mexico—at Las Trampas too—but one feels it particularly here. The Christ on the main altar—supposedly, the miraculous cross of the legend— has a truly Spanish, blood-streaked grimness. The effect is intensified by long red bands and swirls all over the reredos—as if we were truly inside of a palpitating, bleeding heart. Some of the wilder swirls of red paint and carved wood even reminded me of the forms people have called vaginal in the paintings of Georgia O'Keeffe.[1]

That thought stayed with me, a few days later, as I wandered the cool green corridors of the new O'Keeffe museum in Santa Fe. O'Keeffe is a painter easy to underread or condescend to. Her cattle skulls are taken as an obvious memento mori; her oversized flowers are vaginal, to the horror, once, of the squeamish, and later to the delight of some feminists. Her pelvis series, often with a moon showing through the gap, seems an almost perverse fusion of sexuality, death, and birth. But, as the critic Mark Stevens remarks:

> It would be surprising if an artist with her passion for transcendence did not make use of erotically charged imagery. Reducing her flowers to symbols of female sexuality is, however, a trivializing mistake, for the sexual particulars matter less in art with this aspiration than the vivid and more universal sensation of a joyful release into another world beyond the usual distinctions.

To carry this one step further, one might say that birth and death are the two most drastic alterations of our experience of space (and time), "beyond the usual dimensions," that we will ever have to go through, and that perhaps that was what interested O'Keeffe. "Joyful release," it is true, may not be the only emotion. Some of the jimson weeds have cores that almost suggest black holes. But *all* the feelings that are possible in a liminal, close-in place, where "the large [is made] small and the small large."[2] Perhaps, I thought, O'Keeffe's overwhelming purpose as an artist is to destabilize the viewer in space.

Take, for instance, the picture called *Stump in Red Hills*. The flamelike curves of the twisted, constricting wood are huge, leaping from earth to heaven. Not only does the aerial view of the hills in the background make them seem smaller; their softer colors, yellow and yellowish-orange, give their curves a gentle, recessive quality. It takes all one's powers of rational self-correction to retain any awareness that the hills in fact extend themselves enormously through space and would dwarf the tiny stump.

Or take the motif of a vertical line dividing the canvas down its very center. It seems to run through O'Keeffe's work from many periods. In an early painting like *Blue Line*, it is easy to read it as a vaginal symbol—the very abstraction, and sensuous rounding, of the surrounding shapes suggesting bodily curves. But in New Mexico drawings and paintings like *Dry Waterfall*, it reappears as a literal feature of the landscape—a barely perceptible fissure dividing the cliffs and then shaping an arroyo through the talus slopes below—while keeping its formal organizing power. Then in *Black Place III* it leaps back into semiabstraction, with a new and alien mystery. The gray-green hills fold in from the sides to an indecipherable blackness, where an arrow-pointed bright green torrent zigzags from zenith to base. Is it water? Is it, perhaps, lightning from a thunderhead? (The hill-shapes seem to dissolve, at the top of the picture, into a band of white clouds.) Or is it something more purely abstract, a pattern on an Indian pot? Whatever one decides, representationally, there is about this painting a sense of very black places, in the cosmos and the psyche, and the revelations that can happen there, that no amount of familiarity diminishes, for me. It seems most of all, perhaps, like the Pueblo peoples' *shipapu*, the place of emergence of all living creatures, located in the mountains, which is also the place to which the dead return.

Stevens observes that O'Keeffe has "no interest in the middle distance, which is the ordinary measure of human life." Such a lack of interest is, perhaps, the mystic's perspective. What is near at hand is important and requires our attention and care—"Everyday mind is the way"—but its background is always infinity, the first and last things. The middle distance is where we plan, where we look out for the dangers that might be approaching, where we see other people and things in perspective, that is to say, as smaller than ourselves. O'Keeffe's familiarity with Zen Buddhism, and with Asian aesthetics, is well documented. "She appreciated . . . the mysterious sense of infinite space—at once page and sky—suggested but not depicted in Asian art," and "she learned from [it] to dispose of the horizon line"—that measure of near-, far-, and middle-distance—writes Barbara Rose.[3] Mark Stevens draws a perhaps obvious, but important, conclusion about O'Keeffe's choice of where to live. The desert is preeminently the place where the middle distance disappears. "Mystics and hermits are traditionally attracted to the desert for its aura of simplicity, revelation, and death."[4]

Something about space and shape, their ins and outs, their off-balances and reversibilities, and a resulting connection with Last Things, holds these three places, three centers of art, together in my mind. I visited them while I was attending a conference on D. H. Lawrence in Taos in the summer of 1998. I had just heard Sandra Gilbert give a brilliant and somewhat unsettling talk about Lawrence's last poems, and their liminal space between life and death. She talked about funeral flowers, and how they allude to our fear, or hope, that the dead will reemerge, materially, in that shape. A *shipapu* under our very noses, as it were. In the churchyard at Las Trampas, the graves are fenced-in oblongs, the shape of the corpse beneath, and they are planted to the very edge with bulb plants, or large-leaved weeds.

Tamar and Tonalism

In his old age, William Keith—his strokes broader and more impressionist now, his palette brighter—lost his gallery and much of his work in the San Francisco earthquake and fire. Consequently, he and a number of his proteges persuaded the Del Monte Hotel in Monterey to open the first gallery exclusively devoted to California painters. So the Monterey Peninsula had become a center for the visual arts well before Robinson Jeffers settled there in the 1910s. In 1995, the Oakland Museum put together an exhibition of the artists who showed at the Del Monte, under the rubric "Tonalism."

"Tonalism," it must be said at once, is a modern term. The artists would have called themselves "luminists," after the earlier generation of East Coast painters who also emphasized softly radiant seashore light. The term "tonalism," the catalogue tells us, refers to a further dimension of their practice, "subtle nuances of color gradation within a relatively narrow range of spectrum hues." There is a "dominant hue," like a musical key, "with each subordinate hue in the composition harmonized by mixing it with a tinge of the dominant hue."[1] Many of the California tonalists studied in Paris in the 1880s and 1890s and absorbed this approach from the influences dominant there: Whistler, Puvis de Chavannes, the general vogue for all things Japanese. But their particular genius lay in realizing that, in the foggy summers of the Monterey Peninsula, removed from the intense light of the inland valleys, this narrow range of colors reflected how California actually looked: "the faded greens and tawny ochers of the grassy hillsides in late summer, along with the gray-green foliage of eucalyptus, live oaks, and olive trees, blend their muted tones with the pearly grays of marine mists."[2]

In practice, the tonalist painters seem to take two different directions. There is a great deal to remind one of Monet and Turner, as well as Whistler and Inness, in the way hazy or diminished visibility is handled in the wonderful nightscapes of Charles Rollo Peters, or the twilight pieces of Granville Redmond, Xavier Martinez, Sydney Yard. In the Monterey cypresses of Arthur Mathews, by contrast, or in almost anything by Gottardo Piazzoni, color areas are much more distinct and firm; perspective is a little flattened, in the manner of Puvis; so the color "harmony" is both prominent and stylized. Both modes convey an inner landscape, a slightly melancholy protected withdrawal, or a meditative peace, as strongly as they do an outward one; but in the second we are on into the decorative, orientalizing style of art nouveau.

In some of Gottardo Piazzoni's work a further element appears: a sorrowful female figure, standing or kneeling, in archaic or Japanese robes, gives a center to the Monterey landscape and makes it immensely lonelier, "measur[ing]," as Wallace Stevens said, "to the hour its solitude." In *Reflection*, she is poised—as if about to jump?—over the Japanese-perspective downrush of a Point Lobos cove. In *Lux Eterna*, she kneels in prayer, against shadowy hills and an overarching fog bank. In *Silence*, there are two robed figures. One stands by the shore, hazily reflected in murky gray-brown-green water; the other sits some distance away. It is twilight. Behind their small clearing stretches a pathless forest of live oaks, the same color-mix as the sea. A tan hillcrest shows in the far distance, whether as goal or barrier; above it, the eternal fog.

*   *   *   *

Looking at these paintings, I couldn't help but think of Robinson Jeffers. It wasn't just that the classicizing, which makes Piazzoni's paintings so dated, reminded me how Jeffers too staged biblical and Greek stories of incest and family murder in the same foggy canyons. It was also the profounder need for a human figure to center, to mediate, what seems out of scale in the Pacific landscape, including the extreme loneliness of living there, the lack of containing limits to what grief, eros, or violence might occur.

Jeffers said that his narratives grew out of something excessive, "an emotion that seems to overflow the limits of lyric or description," in his reaction to a place. "[E]ach of my too many stories has grown up like a plant from some particular canyon or promontory, some particular relationship of rock and water, wood, grass and mountain."[3]

There is often something painterly about the "particular relationship" between Jeffers's characters and the landscape. At the beginning of "Thurso's Landing":

> The group dissolved apart, having made for a
>   moment its unconscious beauty
> In the vast landscape above the ocean in the colored
>   evening; the naked bodies of the young bathers
> Polished with light, against the brown and blue denim
>   core of the rest; and the ponies, one brown, one piebald,
> Compacted into the group, the Spanish-Indian horseman
>   dark bronze above them, under broad red
> Heavens leaning to the lonely mountain.[4]

At the end of the same poem, Jeffers seems to see the West Coast itself as a kind of theater set, designed to present a fundamental human "mystery" ("final" in the sense of "essential," *because* it is "final" in the sense of being the limit of westward migration) against a backdrop of infinity:

> The platform is like a rough plank theater-stage
> Built on the brow of the promontory: as if our blood had
>   labored all around the earth from Asia
> To play its mystery before strict judges at last, the final
>   ocean and sky

Jeffers's destructive heroines, in particular, appear almost as annunciations of some quality of place. Here is Tamar, her sexuality concealed and emphasized by a setting whose essence is its concealing/revealing reflections and intertwinings:

> White-shining
> Slender and virgin pillar, desire in water
> Unhidden and half reflected among the interbranching
>   ripples,
> Arched with alder, over-woven with willow.

nd here the apparition of the masochistically wounded Fera in *Cawdor*, with the "pillar" metaphor again signaling a pictorial centering, as well as giving the woman a quasi-phallic power:

> like a lit pillar Fera alone
> Waiting for him, flushed with the west in her face,
> The purple hills at her knees and the full moon at her
>   thigh, under her wounded hand new-risen.[5]

This passage even has the tonalist quality of "a dominant hue . . . with each subordinate hue in the composition harmonized by mixing it with a tinge of the dominant hue."

Few people now read Jeffers's longer narratives all the way through, even though the writing is—as I hope these few quotes show—often very compelling. Robert Hass has suggested that they were once more popular largely because, in those days, poets could get away with more than novelists; line breaks induced a curious blindness in the censor.[6] One could unkindly compare the structure of *Tamar* to that of a pornographic novel—a series of increasingly explicit and perverse sexual encounters. Tamar seduces her brother; she seduces Will Andrews; she offers herself

> Gone beastlike, crouching and widening,
> Agape to be entered, as the earth
> Gapes with harsh heat-cracks, the inland adobe of sun-
>   warmed valleys

to the spirits of the old Indian gods during the seance. Finally she exposes herself to, and apparently seduces, her father while invoking *his* dead sister/lover—this fourth sexual act precipitating a fifth violent one, in which all the characters perish.[7]

Jeffers said, famously, that he wrote about incest to allegorize mankind's self-isolation from nature. But in the poem it seems much more a result of isolation *in* nature. Lee Cauldwell's choice is between his seemingly innocent communion with his sister and "loves with dark eyes in Monterey back streets, liquor / And all its fellowship"; otherwise, "what was left to live for but the farmwork . . . ?" His pretext for warning off Tamar's exogamous lover, Will, is that he too belongs to the "old" wicked life Lee has "quit." More interestingly, western nature itself seems to suggest to Tamar that she act on her forbidden impulse:

> Was it the wild rock coast
> Of her breeding, and the reckless wind
> In the beaten trees and the gaunt booming crashes
> Of breakers under the rocks, or rather the amplitude
> And wing-subduing immense earth-ending water
> Taught her this freedom?

This connection appears elsewhere. Two of Jeffers's ambivalent heroines, Fera in *Cawdor* and "Fauna" in that early, never-reprinted poem, have names synonymous with wildness. And it is when Hood Cawdor hears two farmhands speak of the Big Sur coast as a "beautiful stepmother country" that he realizes the danger *his* seductive stepmother poses to him.[8]

Moreover, in *Tamar*, the more manipulative, sadistic, and ultimately self-destructive the heroine's actions become (her villainy strains credulity, if one reduces the poem to a plot summary), the more strongly she feels merged with the landscape, its magnitude and indifference:

> There is the great and quiet water
> Reaching to Asia, and in an hour or so
> The still stars will show over it but I am quieter
> Inside than even the ocean or the stars.
> Though I have to kindle paper flares of passion
> Sometimes, to fool you with.

It is as if the Carmel coast is at once "the world's cradle" and, perhaps because of the finality of its position, for the West, facing "Asia," the site of the world's final loss of innocence: the "age-reddened granite" that "crumbles apieces / Now that we're all grown up." Only the most terrible actions can illustrate how indifferent it is:

> neither glad nor sorry to take the seas
> Of all the storms forever and stand as firmly
> As when the red hawk wings of the first dawn
> Streamed up the sky over it. . . .

That this feeling was Jeffers's, ventriloquized onto Tamar, seems clear enough from the ending of "Thurso's Landing," already quoted, or from "Apology for Bad Dreams":

This coast crying out for tragedy like all beautiful places,
(The quiet ones ask for quieter suffering: but here the
    granite cliff the gaunt cypresses crown
Demands what victim? The dykes of red lava and black
    what Titan? The hills like pointed flames
Beyond Soberanes, the terrible peaks of the bare hills
    under the sun, what immolation?)

Of course, as many critics have pointed out, Jeffers may have had a simpler reason for associating the Carmel coast with incest and immolation. Jeffers's mother was, in some ways, more like a sister. She was twenty-six when he was born; his austere, demanding father was fifty. As a young man, Jeffers lured away and married the young wife of a much older husband; as Robert Hass puts it, "some have guessed" at "an Oedipal conflict" here.[9] Robert Zaller, in *The Cliffs of Solitude*, has done a definitive study of how Jeffers rings the changes on punitive or absent fathers, seductive mothers, quasi-incestuous adulteries, in all his middle-period narrative poems, from *Cawdor* (1928) to *The Love and the Hate* (1948).

Moreover, Una was a kind of other self to Jeffers, as well as a passionate beloved. She made all his clothes for him (trying to make him look like her other hero, Yeats) and would knock on the ceiling with her broom if she heard him stop pacing during his prescribed writing morning. Sisterhood told one dark, partial truth about their symbiotic relationship, while it avoided a darker one. A Freudian will find it easy enough to believe that Jeffers feared avengers, psychic "wolves," in the lonely place where he had come to exercise his erotic freedom. In an early rhymed poem he actually published in the *Carmel Pine Cone*, he wrote,

Let us go home to Paradise,
    O my adored!
There are neither flaming sword
Prohibitive, nor angels' eyes
Jealous of our happiness.[10]

But the metaphors indicate the enormity of the transgression: sneaking in, by the back door, to the paradise the primordial couple had lost. I personally take Jeffers quite literally when he says that he invented stories of sin and retribution as a kind of preemptive psychic magic; that the "tragedy" this paradise cried out for was only contingently distracted from its proper victim, himself.

> I imagined victims for those wolves,
> I made them phantoms to follow,
> They have hunted the phantoms and missed the house.
> ("Apology for Bad Dreams")

Of course, the topic of brother-sister incest has literary as well as biographical roots. As Karl F. Zender points out in his work on Faulkner, it has a strange double valence from the Romantics on.[11] It can stand for the damaging self-absorption of an old etiolated culture, as in "The Fall of the House of Usher" or *The Sound and the Fury*. But it can also, as often in Shelley and Byron, suggest a breaking of rules, a statement of primacy over the older generation, appropriate to the revolutionary founders of a new Eden. It seems fair to say that Jeffers, however unconsciously and confusedly, expresses both possibilities. The incest in *Tamar* does spring from the seductive invitation of "the amplitude / And wing-subduing immense earth-ending water," the West as a new Eden, where old rules do not apply. And it is also a desperate inward-turning, but not one situated, as in Poe or Faulkner, at the heart of an old culture overly proud of its richness, rather in the cultural poverty of the frontier, in a family almost without human or social context, overwhelmed by nature. In that sense, it expresses the panic we have found near the core of the best western writing, throughout.

*   *   *   *

Perhaps the most damaging feature of Jeffers's long narrative poems is not their melodrama but the improbable and intricate philosophizing they force on their characters, especially the labile, destructive heroines. It is no accident that *Roan Stallion* is one of only two longer poems Robert Hass reprints entire in his 1987 selection from Jeffers, *Rock and Hawk*.[12] For in *Roan Stallion* Jeffers succeeds—perhaps for the only time in his career—in balancing a credible plot with a gradual revelation of his metaphysics. On one level, the poem is very much like a well-made short story. The heroine, California, alienated by her husband's sexual exploitation and general meanness, projects her ideal of maleness onto the stallion and then unconsciously maneuvers a situation in which the stallion will kill the husband. It is the kind of "Freudian" story the 1920s liked to tell about its heroines, witness Lawrence's *St. Mawr.* The ending indeed anticipates Hemingway's "The Short Happy Life of Francis Macomber."

But, on another level, California has a parapsychological capacity, which allows the metaphysical to enter the story without ever overbalancing it. Her Native American ancestry serves to make this more plausible. Her very name, and a genealogy that, Jeffers lets us know, includes most of the state's other ethnic strands as well, make her already an allegorical figure. So Jeffers does not have to give her the kind of intellectual self-consciousness he gives Fera and Tamar, to make her emblematize the more "final" human truths, or "new spiritual quantities" (to borrow a phrase from Hart Crane) that may be realized at the end of the westward migration.

California has two visionary experiences, which divide the forward progression of the narrative into panels, like a triptych. The first vision occurs after she prays for divine guidance to cross the swollen ford of the Carmel River in the darkness. The vision seems conventionally Christian, but already it has elements that indicate that California (the woman, and the state) will not separate the light and the dark, the spiritual and the animal, as readily as Christianity does:

> The child afloat on radiance had a baby face, but
>   the angels had birds' heads, hawks' heads,
> Bending over the baby, weaving a web of wings about
>   him. He held in the small fat hand
> A little snake with golden eyes. . . .

Irresistibly, the elements of phallic and animistic power in the vision draw her beyond its anthropomorphic Christian basis, and associate, in her mind, with the noble sexual power she feels in the stallion, in contrast to her husband's boasting and manipulativeness. Telling the Christmas story to her daughter, while resisting her impulse to go watch the horses mating, she makes a number of telling and poetic Freudian slips ("she was the stallion's wife"; "she was not afraid of the hooves— / Hands"). These culminate in a vision of the stallion/god as a kind of Jehovah beyond Jehovah, putting in question all imagistic representation:

"Did God live near her house?" "He lives
Up high, over the stars; he ranges on the bare blue
    hill of the sky." In her mind a picture
Flashed, of the red-roan mane shaken out for a flag
    on the bare hills, and she said quickly, "He's more
Like a great man holding the sun in his hand." Her
    mind giving her words the lie, "But no one
Knows, only the shining and the power."

After her husband goes away, she has the impulse to put her visionary capacities to the test, to see whether "If one should ride up high might not the Father himself / Be seen brooding His night?" She rides the stallion bareback up to the "silent calvary" of the hilltop. Jeffers teases us with the sexual implications of this "ride"; but what the woman finally does—tethering the horse to "the last wind-beaten bush," laying her head down "in reach of the fore-hooves"—is far more restrained, but right, as some of the bizarre versions of the sacred in Flannery O'Connor's short stories seem right. The horse

    backed at first; but later plucked
    the grass that grew by her shoulder.
The small dark head under his nostrils; a small
    round stone, that smelt human. . . .

California does see visions in this posture, both Christian and pagan; but what seems more marvelous to us, and to the narrator, is the "recognition . . . self-equaling, the whole to the whole" between the "microcosm" and "the other extreme and greatness" that this mutual risk across species lines expresses.

Then, too, the place, the Carmel Valley hills under the full moon, becomes an incarnation of the "possible god," as effectively as the horse himself. "Space, *anxious* whiteness, vastness" (italics mine), it contains the terror that is always part of the white man's experience of western loneliness. Yet it is undeniably a sacred place. Too high for trees, it reduces secular things ("woods and valleys") to mere "symbol[s]" of themselves. "Enormous films of light" stream down, as on Danae or Semele; the air becomes "arcs and spires," a cathedral in itself; a view of the ocean is revealed, "Distant beyond conception," a "doubtful world's end." The place seems made for the revelation of a divinity who will be both natural and imageless, "the whole to the whole." And, when we return to the human plot, it is this very quality of divine revelation that leads to tragedy; making the husband's sexual boast— that he will "show you what the red fellow did"—blasphemy, it precipitates the murder.

I was delighted to find that even Jeffers's hilltop scene has its counterpart in the visual art of the period. The moonlight like "daylight," the almost animate "vast round backs of the bare hills," the few live oaks like "little / Darknesses on the far chart," appear in Charles Rollo Peters's *Visitation*, a localized version of the appearance of the angel to the shepherds. The light brings out one same tawniness—almost Jeffers's "anxious whiteness"—on the sheeps' wool, a shepherd's woolly hair, and the summer grass. The angel stands out beyond the "little vapors," in exactly the same position as Jeffers's God who "walks lightning-naked on the Pacific"—a gentler presence, but one which similarly tests received ideas of the sacred against the "doubtful world's end."

*   *   *   *

I spent a frustrating two days in the Harrison Memorial Library's Carmel History Room, and the Monterey Peninsula Museum of Art, trying to establish a more direct connection between Jeffers and the tonalists. Piazzoni summered in Carmel Valley, on his family's ranch, which once occupied most of the slopes of Mount Toro. He seems to have held a running party for local artists; his friends developed the habit of painting, or carving, messages on his studio door when he wasn't at home. One of the inscribers was Ansel Adams, also a friend of Jeffers. Charles Rollo Peters left the Peninsula too early for Jeffers to have known him well, but his son, the stage designer Rollo Peters, attended Jeffers's funeral. There the trail ends. The only contemporary paintings at Tor House are family portraits. As one of Jeffers's sons said, his father liked paintings but wouldn't go out of his way to go to an art gallery or museum.

It remains, then, at the level of analogy. Yet the analogy remains a powerful one, for me, perhaps because it resonates so with Americans' oldest hopes and fears about their relation to their new but stolen land. The West as Paradise, but as forbidden, incestuous paradise, scene of corruption, scene of the death of the old God, before—perhaps—the birth of the new. California killing the stallion that has killed her husband, with "the mask of a woman / Who has killed God." In Jeffers's case, it was clearly a private nightmare; but how hauntingly it carries. Even in his greatest public success, his *Medea*, where he retells an old myth without altering it, his Colchis still seems really Monterey, and compelling because it is that American strangeness. And his heroine, like Tamar, like Piazzoni's *Reflection*, is the anima figure who must both embody, and be driven mad by, its wild loneliness. "Great eyes like stones," "White bones / On the Black Sea shore."[13]

The Persistence of Jeffers

Robinson Jeffers's reputation has been, to say the least, volatile among East Coast critics. Even the best critic of the postwar generation, Randall Jarrell, who was receptive to Whitman and Williams, called him a poet of "great—but crude and approximate—power."[1] But the question for a westerner, I suspect, is not exactly how "great" Jeffers was, or just how one should qualify his greatness, but why he sticks so in our imaginations. The parallel case, for an easterner or a southerner, would be that other defective genius Allen Tate called "Our Cousin, Mr. Poe."

For nearly every important California—or at least Northern California—poet I know has been engaged in some sort of dialogue with Jeffers. Czeslaw Milosz, who argued with his metaphysics in a famous poem, nonetheless admitted that reading Jeffers, after he settled in California, helped him to allow a discursive, even an angry and prophetic, voice into his own poetry, previously shaped by European symbolism and surrealism. Robert Hass, too, was driven to reply to Jeffers—even to bring him back from the dead, to recant his views—but later took the trouble to edit a fine selection of Jeffers's shorter poems, *Rock and Hawk*. Gary Snyder admits to having organized day-long group readings of *Give Your Heart to the Hawks* and other Jeffers narratives; and once, at the Tor House Festival in Carmel, he read "The Excesses of God" so charmingly and benignly, bringing out a shorter, phrasal countercadence, that for a moment it seemed a Gary Snyder poem. William Everson, William Stafford, Diane Wakoski, Sandra McPherson, Jack Marshall. . . . The list could go on. Even the poets who hated Jeffers—Winters, Rexroth—felt compelled to vituperate against him at length, as eastern poets probably would not have.

Part of the reason, I think, is this: Jeffers belonged to a very special class of poets. Even a visit to Tor House tells us so. This is not a house that wishes to protect its owner, with depths, silences, ambiguities. It is a house that wants to speak, as indeed it does speak in the mottoes, the memorable dates, that Jeffers incised into its wood and stone. Jeffers was not one of those poets who wish merely to accumulate good or great poems, one by one, out of the changes of their lives. Rather, he was the kind of poet—as Rimbaud and Whitman were; as T. S. Eliot became, perhaps against his will; as Gary Snyder may be in our time—who makes his life an unchanging symbol, to which the poems append themselves as testimonials, footnotes. In his poem "Rock and Hawk," Jeffers writes:

> Here is a symbol in which
> Many high tragic thoughts
> Watch their own eyes.[2]

This is an instance of what Harold Bloom calls *apophrades:* the poet, late in life, daring to use a great predecessor's style directly, in order to show all the more clearly how he himself has gone beyond it. The predecessor, here, is Una Jeffers's hero Yeats, who was, I think, much more of a model to Jeffers than is commonly realized. But the line only Jeffers could have written is the third: "Watch their own eyes." And it expresses his wish: to be a symbol capable of watching itself, to look back, as it were, from the permanent and resolved part of himself onto the accidental and changing part, as the hawk in the poem seems to enable the rock to watch itself. If Jeffers's deathbed is not, as I once believed, actually built into the stonework of Tor House, it is built into the idea—a finality of meaning beyond the normal reach of mortal flesh.

Consciously symbolic poets succeed, of course, only in so far as what is symbolized matters to others besides themselves. The agon of Jeffers's soul is idiosyncratic in the extreme; but I have already suggested how it mirrored other writers' terror and desire for reconciliation in encountering the landscapes of the West. I would further suggest that it was also typical of a whole movement in Euro-American religious thought over the last two centuries—a thought that has often been carried on through the arts, since the invention of new sects became an unrespectable occupation.

Jeffers's remote, forbidding father was a Presbyterian minister. He brought his son up in a creed that historically held to the Calvinist view on original sin, predestination, hellfire, and our inability to act virtuously except through the arbitrary intervention of divine grace. The Oedipal struggle that, I have suggested, cast such a long shadow over Jeffers's life took a peculiar, but very human, shape where theology was concerned. He conceded everything to the adversary on one level, in order to be able to dispense with him entirely on another. Where the human world is concerned, Jeffers concludes, the Calvinists are essentially right. There, all is violence, lust, and greed, false pride and illusory security. Philanthropy is hopeless in any case, and may itself be merely a subtler aggrandizement of the ego. It all deserves destruction, and it will all be destroyed, by the God of scientific infinities as surely as by Jonathan Edwards's God who "holds [us] over the pit of hell, much as one holds a spider, or some loathsome insect over the fire."[3]

But even on this level, Jeffers's God is less above the fray than Edwards's. He is a self-tormentor, like Emerson's Brahma or Baudelaire's *Heautontimoroumenos*; his victims are only divided portions of himself.

> I bruised myself in the flint mortar and burnt me
> In the red shell, I tortured myself, I flew forth,
> Stood naked of myself and broke me in fragments,
> And here I am moving the stars that are me.
>
> ("Apology for Bad Dreams")

Moreover, once the human level is left behind, another kind of world opens out, for Jeffers, in nature: a world of pure being, beyond gods, beyond struggle or consciousness, quiet yet vibrant with potentiality. It is the "star-color" rock-wall up Ventana creek, "grave, earnest, not passive," in which the "packed centuries" are made visible; it is the old woman, now "a cell of dry skin / Soon to be shed from the earth's old eyebrows," who, because once in her youth she suckled a day-old faun and felt it "Digging its little hoofs like quills into my stomach," has "lived in the streaming arteries, / The stir of the world, the music of the mountain." It is the light-effect at twilight in Carmel Valley, "the splendor without rays, the shining of shadow, / Peace-bringer, the matrix of all shining and quieter of shining." It is the infinite, impersonal cosmos, "out of grasp of the mind enormous," revealed by science; yet the feeling toward it is evidently religious. And this cosmos is definitively feminine, as both the Calvinist God and his opponents are definitively masculine.

> . . . The sun-lovers have a blond favorite,
> A father of lights and noises, wars, weeping and laughter,
> Hot labor, lust and delight and the other blemishes.
>   Quietness
> Flows from her deeper fountain; and he will die; and she is
>   immortal.   ("Night")

This feminine "quietness" not only outlives the masculine "noise" but allows us to see it outside the moralistic or Calvinist perspective, as Nietzsche saw it in *The Birth of Tragedy:* as part of an aesthetic pattern, necessary for the plenitude of creation, and therefore, though evil from a local point of view, from the ultimate point of view "beyond good and evil," like Being itself.

What I am suggesting is that Jeffers's personal conflicts, his struggle with his father, fear of psychic "wolves," and ultimate, though dangerous, allegiance to the feminine as personified in Una, all made him peculiarly suited to be part of the great event of the last two hundred years in the religious life of the West. I mean the turning from theistic, moralistic, pseudofactual modes of thinking to intuitive, contemplative ones, without doctrines or promises; and with them, often, the reawakening of a Great Goddess figure who embodies these modes, as God the Father embodies the opposite ones. Jeffers belongs, with Rilke, with Mallarmé, with Whitman and Hart Crane and D. H. Lawrence, to the great project of inventing a spirituality that can survive the death of Christianity; inventing, as Jung and Heinrich Zimmer said, an equivalent of Buddhism that would not be Buddhism, but something distinctively Western. And what could be more Western than the landscape, "west of the west" as Jeffers put it, which for him symbolized the new revelation; or the language of modern science he made so effortlessly part of it?

Jeffers is nowhere more of a founding figure than in his openness to this language, which almost every other modernist considered antithetical to human feeling. Years before Fermi's chain reaction, the smashing of the atom is his metaphor both for the acts of the self-tormenting God and for the mystical experience of "recognition / Not praying, self-equaling, the whole to the whole." The literal size of the stars figures regularly in his poems, as well as, more traditionally, their seasonal appearances. And this legacy has been particularly taken up by West Coast poets. I think of Snyder's botany and geology; of Carolyn Kizer's poem about Einstein; of James McMichael's accounts of aerospace research and wind tunnels in *Four Good Things*. I think of Sandra McPherson's delicately observed "Fringecups," "so palely, recessively matched to the forest floor," but with "a deep pink sign of aging / on a cup's curled edge," and the meditation on ecological boundaries they provoke; of Brenda Hillman's nerve impulse "like a hiker," that

> climbed
> into blockish boats ("receptors")
> was ferried across the synapse, the little
>
> Lethe between two cells. . . .[4]

Our openness to the language of science testifies, as I've argued, to the greater insistence of the power of nature in western life than in eastern. Its unpredictability, its "unspeakable variety" in Santayana's phrase, can overwhelm and terrify; but it can also model, as the Lake District did for Wordsworth, profounder or calmer "modes of being," "huge and mighty forms, that do not live / Like living men."[5]

Of course, whatever his metaphysics, Jeffers would not have the following he has if he were not also memorable as a *poet*. But he is, and is at his best, a rhetorical poet; and I think this accounts for many of the vicissitudes in his reputation—and, notably, for Jarrell's judgment that, even if "great," he is "crude and approximate." In the 1920s, Jeffers came in a kind of package deal with other free-verse, declamatory poets who celebrated American regions, the rawness and energy of places that had been frontier within living memory—Edgar Lee Masters, Carl Sandburg, Vachel Lindsay. His decline in reputation has been blamed on his opposition to the Second World War; but similar attitudes did not prevent the postwar audience from taking an interest in Allen Tate or Robert Lowell, or even Ezra Pound. I think one must look instead to the new taste that dominated American poetry from 1945 to 1960, a taste shaped by the New Criticism, that preferred strict meter to free verse, condemned any kind of preachiness, and looked in poetry for the minute subtleties of diction, and especially the puns and ambiguities, by which a complex and ambivalent moral awareness was revealed.

Jeffers is not incapable of satisfying even this criterion. The line I quoted a few pages back, "the matrix of all shining and quieter of shining," is a great line partly because one cannot tell whether "quieter" is a noun, signifying active agency, or a comparative adjective, one stage in an infinite gradation from "shining" to silence. But this is not the way he usually asked to be read; so it was only in the 1960s and 1970s, when poets like James Wright and Galway Kinnell defiantly brandished the emotive adjectives and abstractions the New Critics had banned—"lovely," "infinite," "reality," "nothingness"—that he again had a completely fair hearing.

And, of course, the reinstatement of free verse helped. For Jeffers is one of the great practitioners of the Whitmanian long line; perhaps *the* master who most kept it alive between Whitman and the great contemporary proliferation, from Allen Ginsberg to C. K. Williams. Philip Hobsbaum has remarked that one of the great secrets of this line, which determines its pacing, is an unstated "convention . . . that each line should be deemed of equal length. This means that the shorter lines are more heavily stressed. The longer lines, therefore, have more lightly stressed syllables and carry more outrides. These . . . are consequently taken at a considerable pace."[6] Not only do we say Whitman's line

Out of the mockingbird's throat, the musical shuttle

more slowly than

Over the sterile sands, and the fields beyond, where the
    child, leaving his bed, wander'd alone, bareheaded,
    barefoot,

we also give the former line a dactyl-trochee structure as emphatic as that of traditional verse, whereas the latter allows in a proselike, lightly stressed patter new to poetry. And its tone, therefore, has the immediacy of narrative; whereas in the first line we hear a lyric concentration suggesting that the "musical shuttle" may be a symbol, to be taken at more than its reportorial weight. (A particularly attuned reader may hear a return to such lyrical concentration, along with dactyl-trochee, as the second line slows down toward the end: "bareheaded, barefoot.")

In Jeffers's "The Purse-Seine," we immediately hear Whitman's way of making an almost journalistic tone poetry:

> Our sardine fishermen work at night in the dark of the
>   moon; daylight or moonlight

Jeffers does not vary his line length as Whitman does. But his late-line caesura has a comparable effect, creating a dactyl-trochee unit, and investing "daylight or moonlight" with an archetypal quality, cosmic recurrences between which the fishermen must steer their course, beyond their role in the plot. Now listen to how this late-line caesura, and its opposite, a breathless enjambment, are used to enact the motions of the trapped fish, as they

> . . . wildly beat from one wall to the other of their closing
>   destiny the phosphorescent
> Water to a pool of flame, each beautiful slender body
>   sheeted with flame, like a live rocket
> A comet's tail wake of clear yellow flame; while outside
>   the narrowing
> Floats and cordage of the net great sea-lions come up to
>   watch, sighing in the dark; the vast walls of night
> Stand erect to the stars.

If we accept the last line and a half at all, with its suggestion of universal entrapment, leading to the later image of the "wide city" as a purse-seine, I would suggest we accept it first musically—taking pleasure in the unexpected redoubling of the late-line, five-to-six-syllable unit as a line-beginning. (Jeffers's music here, I must pause to say, is marvelous in other ways too. Consider the sound-reinforcement between "destiny" and "phosphorescent," words utterly different in their semantic function—a kind of effect Sylvia Plath, later, would be particularly fond of. Consider the sound interplays in "narrowing / Floats and cordage," the hidden rhyme of "narrowing" with "sighing.")

When Jeffers is in his mode of invective and public grieving, his weariness, disillusionment, and his transcendental long view find powerful expression in the line's tremendous downslope. Here, the Whitmanian mode is joined with Yeats's mode of squaring off an oracular or outrageous statement within the line as within the marble of an entablature.

> The old shepherd Caesar his vicious collies, watching the
>   flock. Inevitable? Perhaps, but not new.
> The ages like blind horses turning a mill tread their own
>   hoof-marks. Whose corn's ground in that mill?
>
> ("Blind Horses")

(The koanlike, unanswered question at the end, turning from condemnation to the mystical, also seems to me particularly Yeatsian.)

Some of Jeffers's most powerful invective occurs in the poems on the Second World War, once suppressed (since Jeffers advocated American neutrality, and did not rank Roosevelt much above Hitler), but now available in Robert Hass's selection *Rock and Hawk.* There are moments of unexpected, though very dark, humor. Having heard Hitler's voice on the radio, he says, "Well: the day is a poem: but too much / Like one of Jeffers's." Or, predicting victory and a *Pax Americana:* "my money on amazed Gulliver / And his horse-pistols."[7]

But none of these purely denunciatory passages quite compares with the moment in "Pearl Harbor" when he simply looks at Carmel in the blackout, or with the heartbreaking "Contemplation of the Sword"—poems touched with personal vulnerability:

> The sword: that is:
> I have two sons whom I love. They are twins, they were
>   born in nineteen sixteen, which seemed to us a dark
>   year
> Of a great war, and they are now of the age
> That war prefers. The first-born is like his mother, he is so
>   beautiful
> That persons I hardly know have stopped me on the street
>   to speak of the grave beauty of the boy's face.
> The second-born has strength for his beauty; when he

strips for swimming the hero shoulders and wrestler
   loins
Make him seem clothed. The sword: that is: loathsome
   disfigurements, blindness, mutilation, locked lips of
   boys
Too proud to scream.[8]

To love Jeffers, one must allow him his limitations. The humor,
and the relish for what Williams called the American language,
in "my money on amazed Gulliver," are rare. Ordinarily, the tone
doesn't deviate very far from a plainspoken, slightly magisterial
solemnity. He is never ashamed to rely on plain, commonly used
adjectives and abstractions—as, here, "grave beauty," "loathsome
disfigurements." His vocabulary, apart from the scientific words,
isn't unusual or innovative. Yet, when one grants all this, the best
of his poetry "lives along the line," with the surprises, the twists
of a unique human voice, the matchings of sound to meaning,
which poetry must have if it is to last. Shards of it stick in one's
mind and turn up years later: "This was the high plateau of summer and August waning."

   A few centuries
Gone by, was none dared not to people
The darkness beyond the stars with harps and habitations.

"A crystalline interest." "Great-enough both accepts and subdues."

Steinbeck, Science, and the Tao

In 1932, a "year of crazy beginnings," John Steinbeck, Ed Ricketts, and Joseph Campbell—the later much-renowned Jungian
anthropologist—were all living in Pacific Grove, and "all reading
the poetry of Robinson Jeffers." They hoped Jeffers, along with
Jung and Spengler, would lead them to a "universal commonalty,"
an overriding vision of "nature power" as "the generator of myth."[1]
Yet the differences, between Steinbeck peering closely into tide
pools, under Ricketts's tutelage, and Jeffers, obsessed with the
stars, are at least as interesting as the similarities. Indeed, one can
hardly imagine two writers, equally determined to put science at
the center of their literary projects, drawing more divergent lessons from it, or more contrasting emotional timbres.

Jeffers's scientific world is one of implacable long-term processes, unimaginable infinites, "crying out for tragedy." Steinbeck's, as set forth in the classic "Great Tide Pool" chapter of *Cannery Row*, is a world of unpredictable short-term adjustments and
balances:

> The lovely, colored world is glassed over. Hermit crabs
> like frantic children scamper on the bottom sand. And
> now one, finding an empty snail shell he likes better than
> his own, creeps out, exposing his soft body to the enemy
> for a moment, and then pops into the new shell. A wave
> breaks over the barrier, and churns the glassy water for a
> moment and mixes bubbles into the pool, and then it
> clears and is tranquil and lovely and murderous again.[2]

As in A. R. Ammons's poem "Corson's Inlet," there is "no arranged terror":

> terror pervades but is not arranged, all possibilities
> of escape open: no route shut, except in
>   the sudden loss of all routes[3]

The violence that does occur can be terribly matter-of-fact: "Here a crab tears a leg from his brother." It can also be terribly skilled and beautiful: the octopus "moving like a gray mist, pretending now to be a bit of weed, now a rock," that "oozes and flows toward a feeding crab, and as it comes close . . . its body turns rosy with the pulsing color of anticipation and rage" (18). (That "rosy . . . color of anticipation and rage" makes me think of Blake's "The wrath of the lion is the wisdom of God." Both writers refuse to separate the beauty of biological energy from its cruelty.)

If "terror pervades," so does sex. The tide-pool world literally stinks with it, and its intertwinings with mortality: "The sharp smell of iodine from the algae, and the lime smell of calcareous bodies and the smell of powerful protean, smell of sperm and ova fill the air. . . . The smells of life and richness, of death and digestion, of decay and birth, burden the air" (18). Yet we cannot simply hold our noses at this incredible distillation of life-energy, any more than we simply feel horror at the "rosy" hue of the leaping octopus.

All portraits of the State of Nature are implied portraits of the human condition. After reading about the great tide pool, we expect a tone of acceptance, pity, and wonder rather than moral judgment, an insistence on what is rather than opinions of what is. We do not expect that people will be blamed very much for the vagaries of sexual impulse; that any absolute lines will be drawn between what goes on at Dora's house, Doc's habit of "help[ing] many a girl out of one trouble and into another" (16), and the happy if impecunious marriage of Mary and Tom Talbot. Nor will we be surprised that Steinbeck has little investment in the work ethic; that "no-goods and blots-on-the-town and bums" are put in the same category with "the coyote, the common brown rat, the English sparrow," loved by "Our Father who art in nature" for their "gift of survival" (9). There is little room, here, for Jeffers's pursuing, avenging God. Ultimately, what this book—like the Tao Te Ching—is most wary of is our habit of believing our own opinions and judgments. "[Cannery Row's] inhabitants are, as the man once said, 'whores, pimps, gamblers, and sons of bitches,' by which he meant Everybody. Had the man looked through another peephole he might have said, 'Saints and angels and martyrs and holy men,' and he would have meant the same thing" (1).

It took me a while to have the temerity to call this ethic Taoist; though when I did, I of course discovered that I was not the first to do so.[4] Steinbeck himself drops the hint, calling the Chinese grocer Lee Chong "an Asiatic planet held to its orbit by the pull of Lao Tze and held away from Lao Tze by the centrifugality of abacus and cash register" (8). Lee Chong *is* a self-interested man, without illusions; yet his bargain with Mack and the boys, which sets the plot in motion, is an almost perfect illustration of Lao Tze's ethics. Hearing that Lee Chong owns an oversized shed called the "Abbeville building," the group of "no-goods and blots-on-the-town" approach him: "'I and my friends thought we'd ast you if we could move in there. We'll keep up the property,' he added quickly. 'Wouldn't let anyone break in or hurt anything. Kids might knock out the windows, you know—' Mack suggested" (6).

From a legalistic point of view—Western or Confucian—the case is clear. Mack and the boys have no claim on the Abbeville building; their implied threats are a crime, and, if caught carrying them out, they could and should go to jail. But Lee Chong knows no good will come of seeing the matter in this light; he capitulates, asking for rent he knows will never be paid, just to "save face." And yet, Steinbeck tells us:

> Everyone was happy about it. And if it be thought that Lee Chong suffered a total loss, at least his mind did not work that way. The windows were not broken. Fire did not break out, and while no rent was ever paid, if the tenants ever had any money, and quite often they did have, it never occurred to them to spend it any place except at Lee Chong's grocery. . . . If a drunk caused trouble in the grocery, if the kids swarmed down from New Monterey intent on plunder, Lee Chong had only to call and his tenants rushed to his aid. One further bond it established—you cannot steal from your benefactor. The saving to Lee Chong in cans of beans and tomatoes and milk and watermelons more than paid the rent. (7)

So the Tao Te Ching advises: "Therefore the Master takes action /
By letting things take their course." And:

> Let go of fixed plans and concepts,
> And the world will govern itself.
>
> The more prohibitions you have,
> The less virtuous people will be.
>
> . . . .
>
> Therefore the Master says:
> I let go of the law,
> and people become honest.[5]

Taoist ethics are, in our current phrase, "situational." So they
are bound to disappoint those who look for an ethics deduced
from first principles. To such readers, Steinbeck is likely to seem
inconsistent, fuzzy-minded, even repellent. Edmund Wilson's in
some ways quite shrewd treatment of Steinbeck in "The Boys in
the Back Room" is a case in point. Wilson perceives how central
the analogies between human beings and animals are to Steinbeck's work. Such comparisons would be no surprise in Far Eastern or tribal literatures, where the commonalities between living
beings are emphasized more than the differences. But from Wilson's Freudian-Marxist-humanist point of view the comparison
can only be reductive, emphasizing the "processes of life itself"
over what "is most thoughtful, imaginative, constructive" in human nature. Lennie, in *Of Mice and Men*, is the true representa-
tive of the animal-human. Therefore, Wilson concludes:

> And it is only, as a rule, on this primitive level that Mr.
> Steinbeck deals with moral questions: the virtues like the
> crimes, for him, are still a part of these planless and
> almost aimless, of these almost unconscious, processes.
> The preacher in *The Grapes of Wrath* is disillusioned with
> the human moralities, and his sermon at the grave of
> Grampa Joad, so lecherous and mean during his lifetime,
> evidently gives expression to Mr. Steinbeck's own point of
> view: "This here ol' man jus' lived a life an' jus' died out
> of it. I don't know whether he was good or bad, but that
> don't matter much. He was alive, an' that's what matters.

An' now he's dead, an' that don't matter. Heard a fella tell a poem one time, an' he says, 'All that lives is holy.'"[6]

But if one looks at the sermon, not for evidence of "Mr. Steinbeck's own point of view" but as a response to a particular situation, it is far from "primitive"—indeed, almost a masterpiece of Buddhist "right action." Grampa Joad has died at the end of the most terrible day in the Joads' life so far—the first day of their journey westward after their eviction. The temptations are enormous—to be consumed with self-reproach at not having been able to take better care of him; to be consumed with impotent rage at the rulers of the darkness of this world; to "curse God and die." To praise the deceased would be hypocrisy, because he was "lecherous and mean"; to deny that the family loved him would be equally pointless. In this hopeless context, the minister's minimal action is just right. Like the Zen teacher bringing down his stick on the floor—though with some crucial help from William Blake—he praises the *thisness* of what is, and in doing so releases his audience from guilt, blame, and rage.

Far Eastern readers have not been slow to grasp Steinbeck's affinity to ways of thinking familiar to them. In the preface to *John Steinbeck: Asian Perspectives*, Shigeharu Yano, pondering why "Steinbeck is so popular in Asia," says: "Were I asked to express this in one word, I should say unhesitatingly, 'compassion.'" He goes on to say that Steinbeck's "Eastern flavor" is equivalent to Buddhist "benevolence," which is "different from the 'love' of Christianity in some respects."[7] The difference, I might hazard, is that Eastern benevolence is a simpler, cooler matter of doing what is most beneficial for everyone; Christian love puts more emphasis on the subjective state of the lover, and therefore (its critics might say) allows more room for guilt and manipulation. Grampa Joad's funeral oration, Lee Chong's bargain, are cases in point.

The other readership that conspicuously dissents from the condescension toward Steinbeck commonly found in English departments is that of scientists. In *Steinbeck and the Environment*, Susan F. Beegel observes—after noting that "if Steinbeck was mentioned at all at Yale in the era of deconstruction, it was with an urbane sneer"—"[i]t seems that in passing through the doors of the laboratory I had entered an alternate world with an alternate canon. The biologists ranked *Log from the Sea of Cortez* and *Cannery Row* among their great books, the works from which they draw spiritual sustenance and a sense of vocation, right up there with Darwin's *Voyage of the "Beagle."* Not to have read them was inconceivable."[8]

I can confirm the truth of this from personal experience. As a Fellow at the Villa Serbelloni, I was under the gentle obligation to make dinner-table conversation, not only with other Fellows from many countries but with the short-term conferees, in a wide variety of fields, who wandered through week after week. Once I shared a table with a group of oceanographers from Argentina and Chile. My companion had the tango as a topic in common; I foundered, until I happened to bring up the *Log from the Sea of Cortez*—a book I, like Susan Beegel, would hesitate to discuss with my more theory-minded colleagues. I will never forget the reverence, affection, and delight with which mention of the book was greeted.

That the *Log* is so popular with scientists in itself refutes the common stereotype among humanists that the scientist is the last defender of absolute truth and rational demonstration. The book—in which Ricketts appears for once *in propria persona*, not under the loving pseudonym of "Doc"—presents the scientific method quite differently, as "little fragments of seemingly unrelated information . . . accumulat[ing] in a process of speculation until a tenable hypothesis emerges."[9] It is moreover—especially in the Easter Sunday chapter—the *locus classicus* of the philosophy Steinbeck and Ricketts worked out together, or the portion of a philosophy they could agree on, which they called "non-teleological," and I have called Taoist.

What Steinbeck and Ricketts seem to mean by "teleological" thinking is the kind of thinking that looks for a single explanation, that explains, really, in order to explain away, and thereby makes blame and judgment easier. "Non-teleological," or "is," thinking, begins by accepting things as they are, and, while not denying causes, looks for them in ever-widening, never closed, contexts. The teleological thinker—to use Steinbeck's own first example—might conclude that people are unemployed because they are "shiftless and negligent." The non-teleological thinker,

WESTERNNESS

68

casting a wider net, would note that during the Depression the employment rate stayed constant, around "seventy percent," and conclude that individual virtue or vice had relatively little to do with the matter (110).

Non-teleological thinking, Steinbeck observes, will seem "cold, even brutal," to many people, because it offers no quick solutions (111). In fact, "quite the opposite seems to be true." Because nothing need be "condoned or extenuated," the door is open to that Buddhist "benevolence" that Shigeharu Yano considers Steinbeck's "Eastern flavor." Steinbeck's own example is touching, and to the point:

> A woman near us in the Carmel woods was upset when her dog was poisoned—frightened at the thought of passing the night alone after years of companionship with the animal. She phoned to ask if, with our windows on that side of the house closed as they were normally, we could hear her ringing a dinner bell as a signal during the night that marauders had cut her phone wires preparatory to robbing her. (121)

Steinbeck sums up all the positions that could be taken on "the badness or goodness, the teleology of the fears," and the tone of "smug blame" that would be likely to accompany them. Then he says, "But one could say kindly, 'We can hear the bell quite plainly, but if desirable we can adjust our sleeping arrangements so as to be able to come over there instantly in case you need us,' without even stopping to consider whether or not the fear was foolish, or to be concerned about it if it were, correctly regarding all that as secondary" (121–22).

"Non-teleological thinking," Steinbeck says, may look at first glance like a simplistic "It's so because it's so." In fact, it is a matter of "accept[ing] the actually relational answer," which "couldn't be anything else unless it comprised the whole, which is unknowable except by 'living into'" (117). In the end, as in the Eastern figure of the net of Indra, "the pattern goes everywhere and is everything" (124), all things being interdependent. Both the conclusion, and the method of "living into" that it advocates, seem anti-intellectual only because they live around the edges of the intellect, attuned to hunches that may be as yet unarticulated perceptions. For Doc, they constitute the true scientific method; and they could not be more congruent with Taoist or Zen thought.

But when all this is said, there are still those readers who will find *Cannery Row* sentimental or pastoral. It sets up an Arcadia, they will say, in which bums and whores are essentially happy, Taoist virtues the core of their lives. Yet to read the book only this way is to ignore a visionary darkness, especially evident in the interchapters—a darkness that somewhere touches most good western literature, as it does most early American literature. A number of critics—notably Louis Owens, whose chapter on *Cannery Row* is called "An Essay in Loneliness"—have noted the amount of sheer grief in the book, the subordinate stories that, unlike the main story, cannot have happy endings.[10] There are the suicides of three discouraged men, recounted in grim detail. There is the painter Henri's hallucination of a "very dear and yet terrible" young man smilingly cutting a smiling baby's throat—an allegory, perhaps, of the happy self-destruction of Henri's own creative impulses, since he adopts so many aesthetic movements that "[i]t is not known whether Henri was a good painter or not" (83–85). There is the story of the half-witted boy Frankie, who steals a clock from a shop display window because he "loves" Doc, but whom Doc cannot save from being institutionalized. But two episodes in particular, for me, sum up the theme, and open onto the strange, almost unsayable, core of the book's religious perspectives.

One of these episodes comes very near the beginning. There is an "old Chinaman" who appears only at the liminal times of dusk and dawn, going down to the water to spend the night collecting we don't know what in a "covered wicker basket." Everyone finds him a little eerie ("Some people thought he was God and very old people thought he was Death"). Only one particularly "brave" boy from Salinas "knew" he must make fun of the old man "if only to keep his self respect." (Steinbeck, like E. M. Forster, is always ready to see the admirable human qualities manifested in actions that seem simply ugly, viewed objectively.) The old man turns to look at him, and:

What happened then Andy was never able either to explain or to forget. For the eyes spread out until there was no Chinaman. And then it was one eye—one huge brown eye as big as a church door. Andy looked through the shiny transparent brown door and through it he saw a lonely countryside, flat for miles but ending against a row of fantastic mountains shaped like cows' and dogs' heads and tents and mushrooms. There was low coarse grass on the plain and here and there a little mound. And a small animal like a woodchuck sat on each mound. And the loneliness—the desolate cold aloneness of the landscape made Andy whimper because there wasn't anybody at all in the world and he was left. (13–14)

What has Andy seen? Is it something the Chinaman himself has experienced, some inner or outer desert, the unknowable private landscape of another life? Is it emptiness itself, like the thousands of miles of ice and snow Tibetan Buddhist teachers tell their students to visualize? Is the single, borderless, engulfing eye a cosmic or Emersonian one, that belongs to everybody and nobody, so that Andy, in the Zen saying, walks "hand in hand with all the ancestral teachers . . . the hair of your eyebrows entangled with theirs, seeing with the same eyes, hearing with the same ears"?[11] Whatever Andy experiences, it is a powerful moral corrective: "Andy was the only boy who ever did that and he never did it again."

The other episode occurs late in the book. Doc is collecting specimens at La Jolla when, just beyond the outer reef, he discovers the dead body of a girl in an underwater crevice. She seems to be looking up at him, her "eyes . . . open and clear" and her "lips . . . slightly parted," her face showing "only comfort and rest." "Just under water it was and the clear water made it very beautiful." "[B]urned into his picture memory," the face "[goes] ahead of him" as he staggers back to shore, and an internal "music sounded in Doc's ears" (67–68).

The girl is a victim of the unexplained violence and tragedy that hover always at the edges of the book. But equally clearly, she is the Immortal Beloved "smil[ing]" at Doc from her amniotic, Platonic otherworld. It is because she is *both* that she sets off the unearthly music that, like an Enlightenment experience, "he could never remember"—the "high thin piercingly sweet flute" that "carried its unbelievable melody" up "into regions beyond the hearing range," even as a bass line carries the "pounding surf-like" burden of contingency and mortality. The unearthly music signals a moment that "breaks the crust" of the ordinary, bringing Doc slam up against the double nature of what is real. (The phrase "the crust to break through," from Jeffers's *Roan Stallion*, was a favorite of Steinbeck and Ricketts, and is quoted at a crucial point in the *Log* [122].)[12] Another crust-breaking moment occurs through violence, and also issues in music. When Doc returns from La Jolla and learns of the disastrous party, he punches Mack in the jaw, then realizes the futility of the act when Mack refuses to defend himself; Doc then hears in his head "the monotonal opening of Monteverdi's *Hor ch'el ciel e la terra* . . . the infinitely sad and resigned mourning of Petrarch for Laura" (81).

All of these episodes seem somehow related to the book's odd closing benediction—the long poem from Sanskrit that Doc reads aloud at the second, successful party. Death and perfection come together in the erotic memories of a dying man:

> Even now
> My eyes that hurry to see no more are painting, painting
> Faces of my lost girl. . . .

The "little world sadness" of the poem reduces all the hearers, including Mack and Dora, to tears; and only the "almost happy" opportunity for a fistfight brings them out of it (117–18). The next morning, while Doc is cleaning up, he reads further stanzas that draw a more and more explicit contrast between the wisdom that can be stated and experience, the "talking of wise men from towers / Where they had thought away their youth" and "the salt of the whispers of my girl." ("The tao that can be told / is not the eternal Tao," Lao-tze famously begins.) At last the dying man's love broadens to an all-inclusive, cosmic love:

> I mind that I loved cypress and roses, clear,
> The great blue mountains and the small gray hills,
> The sounding of the sea. Upon a day
> I saw strange eyes and hands like butterflies;
>
> .   .   .   .

Just for a small and a forgotten time
I have had full in the eyes from off my girl
The whitest pouring of eternal light—   (123)

Louis Owens comments, accurately, "Doc's 'girl' has been the girl
in the tide at La Jolla, and the 'eternal light' has been the momentary vision of the whole."[13] But I can't quite agree with Owens
that the book ends sadly, because of Doc's abiding aloneness. The
wonderfully equivocal last lines carry, for me, a sudden clearing
of vision, like Grampa Joad's funeral oration, or the Zen master's
thump:

> He wiped his eyes with the back of his hand. And the
> white rats scampered and scrambled in their cages. And
> behind the glass the rattlesnakes lay still and stared into
> space with their dusty frowning eyes. (123)

A *thisness*. Dustiness, menace, emptiness transfigured—without
a single explicit word to say how.

"Too Much What They'd Thought"
Some Notes on Southern California

The problem of Los Angeles is that it is a city planned, not a city grown. Such, at any rate, is the argument of James McMichael's *Four Good Things*, that uniquely odd and interesting long poem of Southern California. Los Angeles reversed the usual order of things, in which people gather at a place for some obvious natural reason—abundant energy sources, a river, a sheltered harbor—and then build the infrastructure needed to sustain their numbers. Here, however: "The region was cut off. It needed / fuel and water, power."[1] And the infrastructure existed before the population to justify it. In Pasadena,

> The rails were
> older than the growth that was the only solvent
> business in the place. If those dispersed connected
> cities didn't grow, there wasn't anything but
> piped-in water, rails, electric power. It had to
> grow by filling in. (42)

"It couldn't do that," McMichael goes on, "on the old / fixed lines" of economic cause-and-effect; it had, from the start, to promote itself, to find "more ways to make the land less simply / there and waiting to be bought," so that finally it would bring "its benefits to everyone from / that large trust that this was where to live."

And so the retired midwesterners are lured out to "'do' the state," to take the "'Day for a Dollar' trolleys," the "tours to studios and missions and the beaches." In a curious mirror-trick, what they are in fact "sold" is "themselves and one another": because so many of them are coming there, there must be something to come to.

> They'd seen
> everything and more, and what it came to for them was
> the building that was going on, a growth they could
> explain by all those landmarks and the days.   (41)

Los Angeles as the city of the emptiness of desire, of its circularity. It's a theme we will come back to, over and over again. For the retired midwesterners, finally arrived, sitting in the cafeterias whose "waterfalls and grottos and lanais were less / peculiar to them now," are plagued precisely by the sense that they have already reached perfection.

> Living here was too much what they'd
> thought it would be. The sequences of perfect days were
> unavoidably what they'd come for.

There is always the sense that "They should be making / more of what was there and possible at any / hour in that clear air." In fact, in a sad but inescapable irony, any concrete embodiment of this infinite happiness is already the wrong one: "With all those possibilities / aligned for them . . . / they should be somewhere else since where they were was / old already with their being there." What they have left behind, and try not to regret, in their old "land with its sweet-scented plains," is nothing so simple as rootedness or lived context, though it is intimately related to those things; it is their "fitness to change." "[T]hey'd left more / changes than they'd known they had," and it is "as if they couldn't know / without those changes where they were or what they / wanted in their lives" (41). In the land of perpetual possibility, there is no adequate or significant change; any specific embodiment, locality, identity, is already, in the telling word, "old." Even the architecture is vitiated by being an escape and an allusion: the Spanish style is "old in what it missed, that native aristocracy of / landed dons," while the Greene & Greenes' "oil- and soap-rich clients" wanted mainly "houses that disclaimed the / sources of their wealth" (43).

That this peculiar mode of unhappiness is the result, not merely of human nature, but of planning, is crucial to McMichael's vision. His long digressive section on Pasadena begins with Von Karman and the Jet Propulsion Laboratory because Von Karman's and ky's science is based on the idea of absolute control through ction: that if one could catalogue every variable and calcu- he consequences of every variation in that variable, then one design the perfect technological response, whether it is the It Palomar observatory or the rockets tested in Von Karman's wind tunnels. Such perfection can have disastrous human conse- quences; Von Karman, McMichael dryly notes, had "helped to plan the arsenals of Germany, Japan and / China, Russia, the United States," and so has more than a merely local connection to the "burned skin-grafted veterans" who walk with their nurses in the arroyo behind his lab (39). (Such perfection of prediction is also, finally, impossible—but chaos theory was not developed, or popularized, enough in 1980 for this to enter into McMichael's thinking.)

Finally, in McMichael's understanding, it is no accident that this apotheosis of the principle of planning should take place in Pasadena. It was because "[t]he region was cut off" and "needed / fuel and water, power," that Cal Tech came into being, as an institution where (in yet another mirror game) "[g]eologists and engineers"—pure science and technology—"would / pay for one another's futures" (43). It prefigured, or began, the whole shift from an economy based on raw materials and visible products— those things so conspicuously absent in Los Angeles—to one that dealt in information and prediction. "Pasadena looked the way it did because there had already been a Manchester," as McMichael puts it in his laconic jacket copy. Here—another theme we will return to!—California is the future, but in ways neither Califor- nians nor prophets might find entirely comfortable.

If we left it at this, McMichael's poem might seem anti-Cali- fornian. That it is not is due largely to the extraordinary climac- tic section in which he tries to inhabit his dying mother's con- sciousness as she sits in her house in Pasadena. (The mother's death, and the way in which her terminal illness was concealed from the poet, as a child, are central to the book, and partly explain its preoccupation with planning away the unexpected.) This sec- tion, as I have written elsewhere, is "the emotional breakthrough that makes the rest of the book endurable," asserting a "transfig- uring emotional companionship" with the world, "without com- promising the book's relentless cleaving to the surface of fact."[2]

This companionship is oddly predicated on "pain" because pain "couldn't be planned away from that one body that was living it in / hope," and therefore defeats the defensive distance from the world that planning inevitably imposes. The pain is "worth it," the mother realizes; "[t]here were / people who made it worth it, and the world." And this "world" is, in a very beautiful, and very local, act of reinhabitation, that previously derealized, purely invented Pasadena:

> Nor was it lonely
> here. Her chair. The dressing table. Desk.
> A blue slip cast ware and a single tile.
> Light from beyond the hedges through the mica
> panels in the shade, the lamp arresting it,
> steadying for that last rush of sun that left her wanting
> nothing more   (44–45)

*   *   *   *

Notwithstanding the movies, and the range of brilliant novelists they lured West, Southern California first became a poetic landscape in the prose of Raymond Chandler. Edmund Wilson's eloquent sentences about its peculiar emptiness are echoed and improved on in many of his, but with the wry tenderness of someone for whom the landscape can never be truly empty because he has lived and loved and suffered there. "Far off there was a sound which might have been beating surf or cars zooming along a highway, or wind in pine trees. It was the sea, of course, breaking far down below." Or more quietly, but with a whole Hopper painting in its barely withheld personification, Marlowe bored in his office: "A wedge of sunlight slipped over the edge of the desk and fell noiselessly to the carpet."[3]

Elliot L. Gilbert has captured one side of Chandler's world perfectly when he calls it "a world in which everything is already over and done with." Going through a Chandler story set in a "late-night hotel lobby," "one of Chandler's favorite settings," Gilbert catalogues all the "'end-of-the-world' references" and references "to the hollowness and insignificance of things."[4]

But one could also say, with equal justice, that Chandler's is a world where everything is waiting to happen, though once it does happen, it will already be, in McMichael's phrase, "old." Terry Lennox, in *The Long Goodbye*, who is often the mouthpiece for both a poetry, and a self-pity, inappropriate to Marlowe, has a wonderful apostrophe to "bars just after they open in the evening," "When the air inside is still cool and clean and everything is shiny and the barkeep is giving himself that last look in the mirror to see if his tie is straight and his hair is smooth. I like the neat bottles on the bar back and the lovely shining glasses and the anticipation."[5]

But the magic lies only, really, in the "anticipation." Later on, "the lushes will fill the place up and talk loud and laugh and the goddam women will start . . . making with the packaged charm which will later on in the evening have a slight but unmistakable odor of sweat." In this passage, Marlowe is free to play Sancho Panza to Lennox's Quixote and say: "So they're human, they sweat, they get dirty. . . . What did you expect—golden butterflies hovering in a rosy mist?" (24) But Marlowe, as we shall see, is himself all too susceptible to "rosy mist" and the fear that what lies beyond it will inevitably disappoint. Responding to the suggestion, in *The Little Sister*, that he might be in love with the actress Mavis Weld, he says: "That would be kind of silly. I could sit in the dark with her and hold hands, but for how long? In a little while she will drift off into a haze of glamour and expensive clothes and froth and unreality and muted sex."[6]

Chandler's Los Angeles, then, is both the world "in which everything is over and done with" and the world in which everything is waiting futilely to begin. Again in *The Little Sister*, Marlowe says, "I smelled Los Angeles before I got to it. It smelled stale and old like a living room that had been closed too long. But the colored lights fooled you. The lights were wonderful. There ought to be a monument to the man who invented neon lights. . . . There's a boy who really made something out of nothing" (269).

The city of illusion, again, of promises that will not, or cannot, be fulfilled. The opening of *The Long Goodbye*, too, is filled with references to these signifiers that seem irresistible despite their lack of content. There are the restaurants where people "spen[d] too much money" because they "exis[t] for that purpose and no other"; the "blue mink that almost made the Rolls Royce look like just another automobile," though "Nothing can" (3).

There are the costumes—gaucho, Wild West cowboy—behind which Dr. Verringer's protege, Earl, hides the reality of his helpless dependence. And of course there is the alcohol itself—the paradigm of the magic world that dissolves, or turns to something utterly different, once it is fully entered.

Behind all of this, of course, lies Hollywood, whether as cause or chief symptom. In *The Little Sister*, when Dolores Gonzales replies to Marlowe's tirade against the corruption of Los Angeles, "It is the same in all big cities," Marlowe says: "Real cities have something else, some individual bony structure under the muck. Los Angeles has Hollywood—and hates it" (358). All Southern California has, at this embittered point in Marlowe's career, is its mastery of illusion, of making something out of nothing. Marlowe still has some nostalgia for the old Los Angeles of "frame houses on the interurban line" (357), which for McMichael was only the beginning of the problem. But in contemporary Los Angeles, even the ocean has lost its romance. It is "the great fat solid Pacific trudging into shore like a scrubwoman coming home. . . . None of the harsh wild smell of the sea. A California ocean" (268).

Chandler's disillusionment is, of course, not merely aesthetic, but political. So the time has come, perhaps, to talk about the social world of the California mystery, and how it—and the resultant plots and structures—contrast with those of the British detective story. The classical British mystery—to generalize a little rashly—follows the plot of Greek New Comedy.[7] It is about a will—that is to say, about the imposition of the will of an older generation on a younger. The social structure within which this occurs is rarely questioned, only the rigidity with which it is enforced. (The social world of the British mystery, indeed, often seems limited to aristocrats, poor relations, servants, and one or two comic rustics.) When the restricting father, or his surrogate, is killed, the event—like its archetype, the murder of the primal father in Freud—plunges the world into moral and existential chaos. People discover that they do not really know each other, or themselves. Because the motive for the crime lurks in everyone, everyone suspects everyone else, and occasionally characters are not sure they are not themselves the murderer. Northrop Frye calls this phase, in comedy, the "ritual death," or "sparagmos"—a term that literally refers to the tearing apart of the god Dionysus, but that in Frye means "the sense that heroism and effective action are absent, disorganized or foredoomed to defeat, and that confusion and anarchy rule over the world."[8] Those who are completely within the established order (notably, in the British mystery, the police) cannot extricate themselves from this phase on their own. It takes, as Frye says, a "benevolent grandfather . . . who overrules the action," or even a "redeeming agent" who "actually is divine."[9] In the classical mystery, this is the detective. He is always a little outside the rules of society—unmarried, perhaps a foreigner, like Poirot, perhaps an aristocrat who has refused to live the life expected of his caste, like Roderick Alleyn or Lord Peter Wimsey. Often he has some weakness that brings to mind myths of the maimed god, the wound and the bow—Holmes's cocaine, Gideon Fell's obesity, Lord Peter's shellshock. He is, in short, intimate with the chaotic world as the conventional characters are not. Therefore, like a psychoanalyst, he can localize the source of evil; and in doing so release the younger characters into the world of liberty in which New Comedy traditionally ends, showing them that their desires to control their own lives are—in all but one case—legitimate, and not murderous.

In the California mystery, none of this obtains because there is no presumption that society embodies a moral order worth rescuing. As Harlan Potter, the super-rich patriarch of *The Long Goodbye*, says to Marlowe in their interview, at the center of the book, "money . . . [i]n large quantities tends to have a life of its own, even a conscience of its own." Though in theory "[w]e live in what is called a democracy, rule by the majority of the people," in fact "[t]he people elect, but the party machines nominate, and the party machines to be effective must spend a great deal of money. Somebody has to give it to them, and that somebody, whether it be an individual, a financial group, a trade union or what have you, expects some consideration in return" (233–34).

So the very rich have enormous power, but use it mainly to keep their private lives sequestered. ("What I and people of my kind expect is to be allowed to live out our lives in decent privacy," Harlan Potter goes on to say. "I own newspapers, but I don't like them.") The California rich, as Chandler portrays them, may be ruthless when directly threatened; but most of the time, they literally do not know what their right-hand men are doing.

The Mob has a different kind of power, no better and no worse, secret, and secretly respected. "Organized crime is just the dirty side of the sharp dollar," Marlowe tells Bernie Ohls in *The Long Goodbye* (352). And when, earlier, Marlowe half-heartedly defends Harlan Potter, saying "I don't figure he's a crook," Ohls himself replies, "There ain't no clean way to make a hundred million bucks" (277). The social acceptability of gangsters with a good front and upper-class manners, like Laird Brunette in *Farewell, My Lovely* and Steelgrave in *The Little Sister*, seems to underline the point.

In between the power of the rich and the power of the Mob, the police survive as best they can. Unlike the police in the British mystery—who are representatives of conventionality, simple foils to the more imaginative detective—Chandler's cops are among his most interesting and human characters. They are poor men who have to guard the world of the rich, and they know it. Either they try, in their small way, to be in on the take themselves, or, if they cling to an idea of abstract justice, as Bernie Ohls does, they are ceaselessly frustrated and angry. The unraveling of Chandler's plots generally uncovers a three-way circuit of complicity—the rich, the Mob, the corrupt or helpless police. In doing so, it reveals that no social authority has any moral standing, but, equally, that there is no one to blame, since money, as Harlan Potter says, has a conscience of its own.

Where there is no villain, desire is the villain. Desire is the American Dream, which has dismantled the hierarchical structure (Terry Lennox's vestigial British accent) and replaced it with the never-ending circuit of illusions. Desire is what gets one into trouble, what leads one to take risks and, momentarily at least, to mistake the world as one wants it for the world as it is.[10]

Hence, I think, the ubiquity of the "girldunnit" plot in the California thriller, from *The Maltese Falcon* on. This solution is rare, and almost bad form, in the British mystery. Where issues center around authority, then either its enforcers or the murderous rebellions they provoke are the source of danger—which leads mostly to male murderers. But where desire is the danger, beautiful women are its personification, the ultimate ideal and the ultimate betrayer.[11] In Hollywood, they are the signifier toward which all the lesser signifiers—bars, Rolls Royces, lavish homes that look like movie sets—are pointing. (Of course, this is not true only in Hollywood. As the psychoanalyst Jessica Benjamin points out, the male psyche, for complex reasons, tends to feel that "desire is the property of the object." Men blame women for the "helpless" attraction they feel toward them; so the "idealized, acutely desirable object" is always, also, the "dangerous . . . siren.")[12]

And yet, different as the California thriller is from the British mystery, the detective retains his role of outsider-redeemer. In Elliot L. Gilbert's brilliant formulation, the distinguishing quality of the "Great Detective" is his superior grasp of "reality." In the British mystery, this tends to mean the intuitive dimension— the understanding of other people that enables him to sense who is guilty, who is not. In the American mystery—while this is not unimportant—it is more his understanding of himself, his unique ability to withstand temptation. Gilbert writes of Sam Spade's rejection of Brigid O'Shaughnessy:

> For Gutman, Cairo, Brigid, Archer, and those like them, wanting to do a thing is always a good enough reason for doing it. Such people are ruled entirely by appetite and by immediate self-interest. For them, there's no world but the one their desires make, no unchangeable reality, no consequences they can't devour except the last one, which devours them.
>
> Spade is different. No matter how much all of him may want to, he will not deny reality.[13]

What Gilbert writes of Spade is equally true of Marlowe. He retains his integrity for three reasons. He does not want money, Harlan Potter's universal conscience. (Other characters, those for whom "wanting to do a thing is always a good enough reason for doing it," taunt him for his poverty in every one of the novels.) He will not defer to the semblance of authority where legitimacy is lacking. And he remains sexually uncommitted. Hollywood cannot touch him. He is Odysseus tied to the mast, hearing the song of the sirens but rigidly restrained by his own code. And, of course, in the end he will suffer for it, in his inability to connect with anyone else. We feel little doubt that Sam Spade is right to turn Brigid O'Shaughnessy in. But when Marlowe rejects the two people he really cares for, Linda Loring and Terry Lennox, at the end of *The Long Goodbye*, we feel he may have outsmarted himself with the rigidity of his scruples, locking himself up forever in his shabbier world. Or so the sad last sentences of the book might suggest: "I never saw any of them again—except the cops. No way has yet been invented to say goodbye to them" (379).

Not everyone has accepted the heroic portrait of Marlowe at face value. Some critics have seen him as a paranoiac masochist.[14] Others have tried to "out" Marlowe, and through him Chandler, on the basis, among other things, of the girldunnit plot, and of Marlowe's emotional friendships with men like Terry Lennox and Red Norgaard.[15] According to these critics, not getting the girl is no misfortune for Marlowe because he really wants the boy. All this seems to me undercomplex; powerful, if conflicted, emotions swirl around the women, as well as the men, in Chandler's novels. The grain of truth in this view is that the books recapitulate some very old themes in American literature, those Leslie Fiedler charted in *Love and Death in the American Novel*. One of these is the classic Freudian split between the idealized woman who cannot be approached sexually and the woman who is sexual but bad. (As Michael Mason points out, most of the women Marlowe is sexually aroused by, before Linda Loring, turn out to be murderesses.) The other well-worn theme is the world of male bonding in which men can, temporarily at least, escape the complexities of sexuality and be truthful and honorable—Natty Bumppo and Chingachgook, Jake Barnes and Bill Gorton going fishing in *The Sun Also Rises*.

It must have taken Chandler some courage to develop the male bonding plot as poignantly as he does in *The Long Goodbye*; he had already read some of the gay-bashing remarks about his work when he wrote it.[16] But this is only one of the reasons *The Long Goodbye* is Chandler's most satisfying novel. Another is the way the heroine-villainess, Eileen Wade, includes but transcends the categories we have just described. When she is first introduced, as the culmination of a two-page lyrical-satiric catalogue of "blondes," she seems to embody the indefinable ideal in a way that we are asked, for once, to take completely seriously: "The dream across the way was none of these, not even of that kind of world. She was unclassifiable, as remote and clear as mountain water, as elusive as its color" (90). But as it turns out, her other-worldly quality is precisely the result, and the sign, of her emotional disengagement. As Bernie Ohls trenchantly puns, near the end of the book, she is a "dream girl" because "Some of her was here and now, but a lot of her was there and then" (324). Though she does briefly become the temptress, offering herself to Marlowe and making him feel (in one of Chandler's less fortunate phrases) "erotic as a stallion," it is in a dream, a somnambulistic state in which she mistakes him for someone else (213). In fact, as we learn, she is removed from the "here and now" by her idealization of the past, of her wartime marriage to Paul Marston/ Terry Lennox. Her idealization leaves her unable either to care for Terry in his later, diminished state or to transfer her erotic attachment to her second husband, Roger Wade; and this inability sets the whole chain of catastrophic events in motion.

Eileen, in short, differs from Chandler's other villainesses in that she is a victim, not just a symbol, of the Lacanian emptiness of desire. With her participation, that emptiness becomes a complete, and deeply satisfying, circuit, each character desiring what is unattainable because it is already turned in another direction: Eileen, her past with Terry; Roger (and Marlowe), Eileen herself; Terry, some vision of himself, and of life, that has long since evaporated to mere style.

*   *   *   *

But who, or where, was Raymond Chandler in all of this? It is an interesting question. Like many of the great western writers, he came from elsewhere and had at least a double identity. Terry Lennox, in fact, lived a life much closer to Chandler's own than Philip Marlowe did. Like Terry, Chandler was born in America but educated in England, and he arrived in Los Angeles with a British accent. Like Terry, he enlisted in the Canadian army and had a traumatic war experience; he was the only survivor of an artillery attack on his unit.[17] He even shared Terry's favorite drink, the gimlet. If Terry is Chandler's traumatized, defeated self—the ultimate outsider, the Englishman in Hollywood—he is also in some sense the self that creates. Because he does not suffer the tough guy's constraints against self-pity, he can give voice to the pure poetry of the apostrophe on bars, quoted earlier. One Chandler critic has even suggested that he embodies a peculiar, three-way connection in Chandler's mind between alcohol, Englishness, and creativity: "a 'controlled' drunkenness and ideal of gentlemanliness, which, for Chandler, was somehow specifically *English* . . . was, or could be, connected with the work of creation."[18]

Natasha Spender, who helped take care of Chandler during his desolate old age in London, suggests that he was actually all three of the male protagonists of *The Long Goodbye*. If Terry Lennox represents one side of Chandler, Roger Wade represents another—his rage at the world and at himself. A macho genre writer who loves Keats and F. Scott Fitzgerald, Wade spews anger both at the conventions of his own medium and at the highbrow literary world that defines it as second-rate. Even a short look at Chandler's correspondence and his few critical essays—so ungenerous to nearly everyone—gives one a good idea where this anger comes from. It is Wade who deliberately goes on a bender in order to break a writer's block, as Chandler famously did during the filming of *Blue Dahlia.* And it is also Wade who finally makes drinking a form of "slow suicide," as Natasha Spender says it was for Chandler.[19] Spender's testimony is that, in London, Chandler's "conversations . . . strikingly resembled the dialogue of all three characters in turn," as if he indeed had a triple personality. Spender defines the relation between the three so perfectly one can do nothing, here, but quote: "Marlowe of course represents Chandler's ideal self, the conscience which punished the Roger Wade within him though not without commendation for achievement . . . and befriended the Terry [Lennox] within, not without censure."[20]

All this, I think, adds a deeper level to our understanding of why *The Long Goodbye* is Chandler's masterpiece. It is not just because it is his best-plotted book, with the fewest loose ends; or because the male bonding plot has an emotional gravity it lacks elsewhere; or because Marlowe loses something of significance; or because the circle of empty desire is completed, giving it tragic stature, and mitigating, to some degree, the scapegoating of the woman. It is also because Chandler found a way, for the first time, to tell the complete story of who he was, in his chosen landscape.

* * * *

Frank Bidart—a forty-year resident of Cambridge, Massachusetts, and, famously, Robert Lowell's literary executor and editor—does not seem the likeliest poet to juxtapose with Raymond Chandler. Yet when we hear Bidart's speaker saying, at the beginning of "California Plush,"

> The only thing I miss about Los Angeles
>
> is the Hollywood Freeway at midnight, windows down
>> and
> radio blaring
> bearing right into the center of the city, the Capitol Tower
> on the right, and beyond it, Hollywood Boulevard blazing
>
> —pimps, surplus stores, footprints of the stars

and then evoking, bitterly but wistfully,

> the stack where lanes are stacked six deep
>
>>> and you on top; the air
>>> now clean; for a moment weightless
>>> without memories, or
>>> need for a past[21]

we could with only a slight stretch of the imagination be listening to Philip Marlowe.

Bidart, who, unlike Chandler, is unequivocally gay, never makes Woman the scapegoat, or image, for the dangers of desire. What he emphasizes instead—as, indeed, Chandler and McMichael both do, in their ways—is the temptation, in a wholly invented environment, to believe that one can have whatever one wishes, that the "past," in the sense of karma, can be left behind. This is, as Nicholas O. Warner reminds us in his essay on Chandler, a crucial aspect of the Hollywood, or the Southern California, dream—the "tantalizing promise of escape from poverty, pain, or the past."[22]

So the danger, for Bidart, is his characters' belief that, like the speaker "weightless" on top of "the stack," they can be anything, regardless of contradiction, regardless of history. The bad taste of a restaurant in Bishop lies in the assumption that you can have everything at once—

plastic doilies, papier-mache bas-relief wall ballerinas,
German memorial plates "bought on a trip to Europe,"
Puritan crosshatch green-yellow wallpaper

                              ("California Plush")

So it is not simply bad taste; its omnivorousness "ha[s] its congruence with / all the choices creating / these people, created / by them." It is congruent, first, with the speaker's alcoholic father, who is constantly lamenting that he cannot convincingly slip into other invented identities, "movie star, / cowboy, empire builder" ("Golden State"). Another, more drastic, indeed Chandleresque, attempt to deny karma emerges in "California Plush" in the story of Wally du Bois, who, at the end of a drunken party, accidentally runs down one of his own guests, then takes the body to a deserted road and "r[uns] back and forth over it several times." In a letter from prison, quoted in its entirety, Wally says, "This sure did teach me a lot of things that I never knew before," and then, "I am a little nervous yet." But when he is released, the nervousness wins out over the fragilely acquired wisdom. Finding that his only son has died of typhoid in his abscnce, he "continued to drink, and as if it were the old West / shot up the town a couple of Saturday nights."

Bidart's California sequence was written while he was still a graduate student at Harvard. So its story is still largely the story of how "I made myself an Easterner, / finding it, after all, more like me / than I had let myself hope" ("California Plush"). There is a certain amount of youthful self-righteousness in the poems' suggestion that only westerners deceive themselves, or fail to learn from experience. The poems idealize not only Cambridge, where "the lovely congruent elegance / of Revolutionary architecture, even of / ersatz thirties Georgian" seems "to bode order and lucidity," but the saving power of philosophical "insight" and—implicitly psychoanalytic—"change" ("California Plush"). Not only does Bidart seem unpleasantly sarcastic in his treatment of his father ("And that was how experience / had informed his life" ["California Plush"]); he also seems vastly overconfident in his suggestion that California's "poverty of history" is the problem, that "awareness of / the ways men have found to live" ("Book of Life") would have been sufficient to save his characters from their fate. All of Bidart's later work, one might say, is the slow, and paradoxically liberating, unraveling of this confidence. But well before the end of the California sequence, one can see the doubts creeping in. The poet dreams of a "stage . . . labelled / 'Insight,'" but "The actors there / had no faces" ("Golden State"). By the end he can even acknowledge that his father has something his own chosen persona cannot encompass or pigeonhole, "the dazzling, impenetrable, glitter of mere life" ("Golden State"). And he must, of course, also acknowledge that it is California, not Cambridge, that has given him his rich and original poetic vein.

Bidart and McMichael do not loom very large on most maps of California literature, at least those drawn by Californians. Perhaps they are simply too critical, too unassimilable to Everson's "archetype"; though Bidart's deliberate self-exile to the East can't have helped. But I suspect that the dryness and spareness of Bidart's, and McMichael's, styles also plays a role. For some readers—and not just western readers—their bareness and prosiness put in question whether they are poets at all. In McMichael's case, it is the endless outpouring of facts, the extremely long, stretched-pentameter lines characteristically enjambed on "a," "the," "to," or "of." In Bidart's, it is the abstract, yet almost chatty, intellectual's tone, the puritan sparingness with imagery. But in the Southern California context, these choices can be seen as acts of stoicism and resistance, comparable, almost, to Philip Marlowe's. They resist an impulse to glamorize as embedded in the lyric tradition as it is in Hollywood, or Southern California real estate. The briefly ecstatic tone of the beginning of "California Plush" suggests how easily Bidart, like his family, could give in to this impulse, if he let himself. "Self-Portrait, 1969," written shortly after the California sequence, ends:

> Sick of being decent, he craves another
> crash. What *reaches* him except disaster?

In McMichael's case, one feels, what the merciless factuality and the seemingly random transitions, the unending digressiveness resist is anything like the planning impulse in himself. Any suspicion of hierarchy—even to the extent of ending a line on a significant word—is too much. It is only when one has completely exorcised the notion that some experience is intrinsically more poetic than other experience that "the world at large"—as McMichael entitled his new and selected poems—the world the dying mother sees, can be enough.

The temptation, it seems to me, for lesser Southern California writers has been to have it both ways, in style and in their attitude toward their native place. They maintain enough irony to establish their elite, or left-wing, credentials, while at the same time subtly conveying that it is really cool to live at, or near, the center of (manufactured) popular culture. It is a characteristically American pitfall, that of the anti-intellectual intellectual. (It does *not* apply so damagingly to Chandler, because his love and his hate both are from the heart; he is not looking back over his shoulder to see what anyone else thinks of him.)

Bidart and McMichael have taken a different, and a very honest, approach. They convey the strength of the Hollywood myth precisely by the severity with which they refuse it. In bringing an unexpected strangeness and dryness to Southern California literature, they have brought an exciting new possibility.

Highway 66

It is an icon of American culture, beginning with the famous song, written just after the Second World War by an ex-marine driving to Hollywood, seeking his fortune as a songwriter. Recently the California *AAA* magazine, *VIA*, printed an affectionately tongue-in-cheek piece called "Get Your Kitsch: Route 66 Turns 75," in which the sights to be seen were, primarily, the most venerable of the tourist facilities, notably the Wigwam Motel in Holbrook, Arizona, a dozen or so stucco teepees in a semicircle that travelers, especially children, found irresistible.[1]

In Steinbeck's *The Grapes of Wrath*, of course, it is the *Via Crucis*—as it was for thousands of penniless Okie families seeking the promised land of California. Every overheated mile tests the failing strength of the Joad grandparents, and the weaknesses of their truck with its wired-together engine. Every turn of the road may conceal a cheating merchant or an unfriendly policeman. The highway is etched in the white American consciousness by pain, as well as by nostalgia.

It figured in my childhood, too, in a gentler way, from the 1940s on. If my parents elected to take the "Southern Route," rather than the Lincoln Highway straight from Chicago to San Francisco, on our summer trips, it meant we would travel more slowly, and eat better food. (I remember the Harvey Houses, and a restaurant my parents somehow knew about in a Mexican hamlet outside of Las Cruces, where the only thing mild enough for me to eat was the tortillas.) It meant we would be more curious about the landscape around us. It meant wonder, though a wonder always somehow hard to seize, hiding further depths: the store in Albuquerque where you could look down through a hole in the floor at Navajo craftsmen, actually making the fine silverwork on sale above. And scary, too: the actual centipede that slowly swerved around the legs of my lawn chair, in Arizona, when I was four.

Then there is Edward Hopper's *Western Motel*, a picture I've always liked, slightly misremembering it, for the memories it calls up of those early trips. The end of the day, the exhaustion and exhilaration of being in this place one couldn't have predicted. And the slight nowhereness of this motel, like all others. Though perhaps, in Hopper's painting, it's actually the beginning of the day, as Gail Levin suggests: the suitcases are packed, the car waiting outside.[2] In any case, a thin line of yellow light, early or late, lies along the top of the bulky nearer hills, while the flat mesa above them is totally dark. There is something mysterious, unreachable, for good or bad, about those hinterlands, but the woman in the room doesn't look at them. She looks blankly out toward the viewer, which is part of the painting's sadness.

Still, it's a shock, for a Euro-American, to see the highway through the eyes of Tayo, the mixed-blood World War II veteran who is the protagonist of Leslie Marmon Silko's *Ceremony*. Behind the two-dimensional spectacle contrived for the tourists who "liked to see Indians and Indian dances," Highway 66 is, quite simply, Hell. "There were Zunis and Hopis there too, even a few Lagunas. All of them slouched down against the dirty walls of the bars along Highway 66, their eyes staring at the ground as if they had forgotten the sun in the sky; or maybe that was the way they dreamed for wine."[3]

But the highway is more than a temptation to Indians to get drunk and lose their souls and their heritage.[4] It is the epitome of the superficiality and destructiveness of Euro-American culture— a strip of speed, waste, and glitter laid down across the "stolen" land. Any sense of "comfort" Tayo might take from the land is "burned away by the glare of the sun on tin cans and broken glass, blinding reflections off the mirrors and chrome of the wrecked cars in the dump below" (117). Looking down on the highway at night, he says, "They took almost everything, didn't they?" (127). And even the wiser Betonie, the old healer, "staring at the lights down below, following the headlights from the west until they were taillights disappearing in the east," can only say, "There are no limits to this thing" (132).

At times, this aspect of *Ceremony*'s vision seems, for lack of a better word, racist. One of the myths old Betonie tells proposes that, as in the Black Muslim story, the world was originally inhabited only by people of color, and white people were invented by an evil magician, just to make mischief. When Tayo returns from the first phase of his healing, his freshened vision sees the white world of the highway in exactly these terms, as a kind of witchcraft, an antinature:

> He stared at the calendar for a long time; the horse's mane was bleached white, and there was no trace of dust on its coat. The hooves were waxed with dark polish, shining like metal. The woman's eyes and the display of her teeth made him remember the glassy eyes of the stuffed bobcat above the bar in Bibo. The teeth were the same. . . .
>
> He wanted to laugh at the station man who did not even know that his existence and the existence of all white people had been conceived by witchery. (154)

Tayo's cure will be, in large measure, a reinhabitation of the traditional Indian relation to landscape. When he and Betonie set out into the Chuska Mountains, he finds himself in a world where the signs of white intrusion have vanished. "He could see no signs of what had been set loose upon the earth: the highways, the towns, even the fences were gone." It is a world that has come alive to the senses ("The mountain wind . . . smelled like springs hidden deep in mossy black stone") and is connected to the infinite ("The world below . . . was dwarfed by a sky so blue and vast the clouds were lost in it"). He feels that "This was the highest point on the earth," in a sense that "had nothing to do with measurements or height" (139).

After the night of the ceremony, his reinhabitation enters a further phase, when he "remember[s] the black of the sand paintings" and sees that the "hills and mountains" he is actually looking at "were the mountains and hills they had painted in sand." This coinciding of the ritual and the real world brings a further sense of infinitude: "there were no boundaries. . . . The mountains from all the directions had been gathered there that night" (145).

Here, as I infer from a number of sources, we have arrived at

a delicate but core issue in the Indian view of the world: the inte
penetration (really, on some level, the unity) of landscape and t
stories about landscape. Silko writes in her essay "Interior
Exterior Landscapes":

> location, or place, nearly always plays a central role in the
> Pueblo oral narratives. . . . [T]he places where the stories
> occur are precisely located, and prominent geographical
> details recalled, even if the landscape is well known to lis-
> teners, often because the turning point in the narrative
> involved a peculiarity of the special quality of a rock or
> tree or plant found only at that place. Thus, in the case of
> many of the Pueblo narratives, it is impossible to deter-
> mine which came first, the incident or the geographical
> feature that begs to be brought alive in a story that fea-
> tures some unusual aspect of this location.[5]

David Abram, in his fascinating book about the contrasting metaphysical assumptions of oral and literate cultures, *The Spell of
the Sensuous*, makes the same observation about Apache storytelling, and connects it with another traditional culture halfway
around the world, aboriginal Australia. Abram calls the relation
between landscape and story in the Australian Dreamtime stories
"reciprocally mnemonic":

> First, the spoken or sung Dreamings provide a way of
> recalling viable routes through an often difficult terrain.
> Second, the continual encounter with various features of
> the surrounding landscape stirs the memory of the spoken
> Dreamings that pertain to those sites. While the sung sto-
> ries provide an auditory mnemonic for orienting within
> the land, the land itself provides a visual mnemonic for
> recalling the Dreamtime stories.

But, of course, what is at issue here goes far beyond a mere mem-
ory-aid. "The land itself" becomes "the most potent reminder"
of the people's deepest "teachings." The people move in "a
linguistic-topological field," "a material landscape *whose every
feature was already resonant with speech and song!* [italics
Abram's]."[6] It is an experienced unity between the human and
the nonhuman, the material and the mental, nature and culture,

unavailable to the Western mind. "This rock's *me*," says one of the Aborigines Abram quotes (168).

It is this unity of landscape, story, and self that Tayo must live his way into through the rest of the book. When Betonie tells him that the traditional ritual alone is inadequate, he gives him a further task within the real world: "'Remember these stars,' he said. 'I've seen them and I've seen the spotted cattle; I've seen a mountain and I've seen a woman. . . . It's up to you'" (152).

And so Tayo sets out on a quest to recover his uncle's spotted cattle, lost while he was away during the war. He spots the constellation Betonie has drawn for him in the autumn sky and follows it north to Mount Taylor, the preeminent sacred mountain in the Laguna culture. There he begins to meet characters who have, to put it minimally, a supernatural aura or dimension. He has a sexual encounter with a woman named Ts'eh. Betonie's stars seem to stand directly over her house. While he is with her he remembers the Laguna ceremony in which the Ka't'sina return to the pueblo, at the same time of year. She has a companion, a hunter, who appears in both mountain lion and human form. Both play crucial roles in helping Tayo succeed in his quest; Ts'eh, apparently, has the power to start and stop a snowstorm by unfolding, then refolding, her storm-cloud blanket. Her nickname ("because my Indian name is so long") suggests both "Tse-pi'na," the Laguna name for Mount Taylor, and "Ts'its'tsi'nako," Thought-Woman herself, the creator figure who calls the world into being by narrating it.[7] When she gives herself a surname, "Montano," "Tayo couldn't remember hearing of that family" (223), and it is no wonder: the name suggests the sacred mountains, homes of the Ka't'sina, and the limits of the world that properly belongs to the people, in all the traditional Southwest cosmologies.

Tayo has, at this point, himself become a character in a traditional story, or perhaps in more than one. Louis Owens has cited the story of the sexual rivalry between Summer and Winter over Yellow Woman. (The mountain lion/hunter figure is associated with winter, and Ts'eh will spend the following summer with Tayo in the southern part of the reservation.)[8] Another myth is offered within the novel itself. As Tayo ascends the mountain to recover his cattle from the white rancher Floyd Lee, Sun Boy has gone to the mountains to win the storm clouds back from the gambler

Kaup'a'ta. As Tayo is helped by Ts'eh, Sun Boy is helped by Spiderwoman, another name for Thought-Woman, Ts'its'tsi'nako.

Perhaps what myth Tayo is reenacting is less important than his feeling that he *is* inhabiting a myth, that he has reentered Thought-Woman's traditional realm, where telling a story can make it happen. "[S]uddenly Betonie's vision was a story he could feel happening—from the stars and the woman, the mountain and the cattle would come" (186).

Just before his agon, when he must confront Floyd Lee's agents and steal back the cattle, Tayo has an experience of an eternal present, something like Mircea Eliade's "mythic time," in which the time of the stories, the human past, and the present are all simultaneous: "The ride into the mountain had branched into all directions of time. . . . The ck'o'yo Kaup'a'ta somewhere is stacking his gambling sticks and waiting for a visitor; Rocky and I are walking across the ridge in the moonlight; Josiah and Robert are waiting for us. This night is a single night; and there has never been any other" (192).

Perhaps the recovery of this vision, through landscape, is Tayo's ultimate victory, which makes all the others possible. Just as the ultimate tragedy, for tribal peoples, may not be the loss of the land itself so much as the loss of a unity, an identity, that can only come to pass in relation to the land. "To force them from their native ecology," David Abram writes, "is to render them speechless—or to render their speech meaningless—*to dislodge them from the very ground of coherence.* It is, quite simply, to force them out of their mind."[9] Just so Tayo has been quite literally forced out of his mind, experiencing himself as "white smoke" that "had no consciousness of itself," in the "white world" of the Veterans' Hospital (14).

*   *   *   *

Highway 66. . . . Where, one wonders, in what hall of the immortals, will the different places it is, geographically identical, ever be seen as one? Will Hopper's sadness then partly be understood by the fact that we have laid down our love of speed, our yearnings, over a landscape that did not belong to them? Will the Indians' outraged desolation be tempered, even a little, by knowing that these satanic, denaturing motel rows were for us a mode of love? (As Louis Owens says, along with "Indian hating," "an unmistakable yearning to *be* Indian [in white American consciousness]—romantically and from a distance made hazy through fear and guilt—compounds the complexity."[10] One has only to remember the Wigwam Motel.) And what, too, of the Joads, who had neither the Indians' sense of belonging nor the middle-class white's privileged nostalgia, but memorized the same deserts and mountains through suffering? As indeed, all of these modes of vision and love are also modes of suffering, in the Buddhist sense, the *dukka* that goes with either trying to hold onto what one is, or to have what one is not.

Perhaps there is no answer. After all, much of human history is shared places, migrations, conquests. Romans and Carthaginians; Visigoths and Romans. The Mexicans who cannot be stopped from pouring north over the border will change the landscape again, and are already giving Anglos their own sense of angry secondariness.

Or perhaps the beginning of an answer can be found in Silko's own emphasis on hybridity. Betonie is an innovative, nontraditional healer, in contrast to Ku'oosh, who starts Tayo on his journey but cannot guide him all the way. Just as Betonie's hogan looks out over the hell-world of Gallup, so his ceremonies make use of elements from white culture. The interior of the hogan is divided according to where the light falls, in sectors Tayo recognizes as traditional and sacred. But while some of these sectors contain "medicine bags and bundles of rawhide," traditional "paraphernalia," others contain "brown, barricading piles of telephone books with the years scattered among cities" and "layers of old calendars." "In the old days," Betonie says, "a medicine person could get by without all these things. But nowadays . . . " (120–21).

Moreover, though Betonie is the source of the embittered myth about the invention of white people, he also tells Tayo, "you don't write off all the white people, just like you don't trust all the Indians" (128). He repeatedly warns Tayo that Indians are trapped when they let their anger against whites become all-absorbing. And indeed, in the unfolding of the plot, it seems that the characters who hate whites the most, like Emo, are also the characters who hate themselves the most because they value only the things that white culture has.

But even more important, nearly all of Tayo's spiritual helpers are, like himself, mixed-blood. He is sexually initiated by a Mexican dancer called the Night Swan, who seems to have quasi-magical powers, and who has moved near Laguna to live within sight of Mount Taylor. She is the first to give him a positive sense of his own mixed identity, saying: "Indians or Mexicans or whites—most people are afraid of change. They think that if their children have the same color of skin, the same color of eyes, that nothing is changing. . . . They blame us, the ones who look different." And she is the first to give him the sense that he belongs to a story larger than himself: "remember this day. . . . You are part of it now" (100).

When Tayo encounters Betonie, he immediately notices that "his eyes . . . were hazel like his own." Betonie replies, "My grandmother was a remarkable Mexican with green eyes" (119). The more we learn about this grandmother, the more uncannily she resembles the Night Swan. She too has appeared mysteriously out of nowhere, near Tse-pi'na, Mount Taylor. And she too is an advocate of "change." She embodies the "transition" Betonie's grandfather has been waiting for, and it is she who persuades him to change, even hybridize, the ceremonies: "We must have power from everywhere. Even the power we can get from the whites" (150).

There are times, indeed, when all the female guardians in the book seem not distinct individuals but avatars of a single goddess. All are associated with Mount Taylor, water or rain, and the color blue. All appear when the male characters need to take some decisive step in defining (and hybridizing!) their identities. And even Ts'eh, though fully Indian, has the characteristically lighter "ocher eyes" (177).

The Night Swan's final contribution is to persuade Tayo's uncle, Josiah, to buy the Mexican spotted cattle—another emblem of hybridity and change. Moving "like deer" (197), they belong partly to the wild nature the Indians revere. They can survive in the desert, even during a drought, unlike the Herefords the white-authored textbooks recommend. Yet Josiah intends to crossbreed them with Herefords, producing a better kind of beef cattle that are at the same time adapted to "Indian land." His project embodies a middle way between Indian traditionalism and Rocky's blind faith in the advice given by whites. Perhaps that is why the recovery of the spotted cattle is so important—indeed, in *Ceremony*'s interconnected cosmology, seems to cause the end of the drought, the regeneration of the land.

But the ultimate hybrid in *Ceremony* is, of course, the text before us. It can be seen as a Western "novel" inscribed within an Indian ceremony. It begins and ends with ceremonial words, set up on the page as poetry. As Louis Owens has pointed out, the opening page, ascribing the story to Thought-Woman, the Indian creator figure who narrates the world into being, makes Silko less than a Western "author" while making the story more than a Western story, a kind of magic, a spell to change the world. Owens writes, "By announcing in what amounts to textual superscript her own subordination as author to the story-making authority of Thought-Woman, or Spider Woman ('I'm telling you the story / she is thinking'), Silko effects a deft dislocation of generic expectations, placing her novel within the context of the oral tradition and invoking the source and power of language found within that tradition. . . . As a result, *Ceremony*, more than any other novel I know of, approaches the category of 'authorless' text."[11]

But it is equally possible to see *Ceremony* the other way around, as an Indian myth inscribed within a high modernist novel. The similarities stare one in the face, if one has taken off the tinted glasses of identity politics. The method of laying a mythic story alongside a contemporary one, so that the latter reenacts the former, is Joyce's in *Ulysses.* The presentation of a mentally disturbed protagonist's past in fragments, faithful to his limited ability to integrate or else tolerate them, belongs to the masterpiece of American stream-of-consciousness, the Benjy and Quentin sections of *The Sound and the Fury.* The presence of characters who are "not wholly distinct" from each other, and ambiguously human and divine, is at the formal core of *The Waste Land,* and of at least two of the modernist long poems written in reaction to it, Williams's *Paterson* and Crane's *The Bridge.*[12] An essay could, and should, be written on why high modernist techniques have remained rich and viable for "ethnic" writers (I think

also of Maxine Hong Kingston, and Toni Morrison), at a tim
when "mainstream" fiction has abandoned them, in favor eith
of a return to realism or the self-conscious gamesmanship of th
postmodern. (Such an essay would probably please no one.)

As it is, other Indian writers have not always been please
with Silko's kind of hybridity. Jana Sequoya and Paula Gunn
Allen have both criticized her, in the strongest terms, for incor-
porating traditional stories into a Western genre available to a
mass (white) audience. "The story she lays alongside the novel is
a clan story, and is not to be told outside the clan," Gunn Allen
writes, and goes on to add the gratuitously *ad feminam* remark,
"Perhaps her desire to demonstrate the importance of breeds [*sic*]
led her to do this."[13] And Jana Sequoya suggests that the traditional stories may themselves be damaged, "confused . . . and
hence forgotten," when they are told "outside the sanctions of
their context," because "in the secular domain of the novel they
are just 'entertainment.'"[14]

It would be presumptuous for an outsider to pass any kind of
judgment on the Pueblo code of secrecy or on conclusions derived
from it. But from the Euro-American perspective, there's something unthinkingly trivializing about referring to our genres as
"secular" and "just 'entertainment.'" Since the Romantic movement, novels and poems have often been regarded as wisdom texts
in European and Euro-American culture. They have filled a gap
between what is perceived as an increasingly fossilized Christianity and secular technological materialism. High modernist difficulty has even made them, in a sense, ritual objects, requiring ini-
tiatory preparation. So that a blending of high modernist novel
and Laguna ceremony is a transaction between two different con-
cepts of the hieratic, not an appropriation of the sacred by the
profane.

But Silko has already built her own apologia into the novel, in
the figure of Betonie himself. Betonie hints that he has been accused of witchcraft, as, Gunn Allen tells us, western anthro-
pologists have been, when they tried to learn too much about
"medicine" lore. But Betonie insists that Indian conservatism is
a self-destructive force, and even serves the ends of "witchery."
"She [his grandmother] taught me this above all else: things which
don't shift and grow are dead things. . . . Witchery works to scare

people, to make them fear growth. But it has always been necessary, and more than ever now, it is. Otherwise we won't make it.
We won't survive. That's what the witchery is counting on: that
we will cling to the ceremonies they way they were, and then
their power will triumph, and the people will be no more" (126).

What we hold in our hands, when we finish this book, is a ceremony that has shifted and grown, becoming a modernist novel
in the process—and therefore, in Betonie's terms, an effort on
behalf of the people's survival. Betonie says of his grandfather,
"He reasoned that because it was set loose by witchery of the
whole world, and *brought to them by the whites* [italics mine],
the ceremony against it must be the same" (150). Not the least
interesting aspect of this sentence is its subtle revision of the
mythology promulgated earlier. The "witchery" is now "brought
. . . by the whites"; it is neither uniquely their creation, nor their
demonic essence. It would seem as though, in producing this hybrid ceremony, Silko has resolved her own internal quarrel between
exclusionary bitterness and an impulse toward the universal.

Thiebaud and the City

The great one in the Oakland Museum is called *Urban Square*. The title is already funny, because what the painting shows is not an open space within a city, but an incredibly crammed closed space—a block, many blocks really, but the intervening streets are crowded out by the perspective—rising between streets exaggeratedly steep, even for San Francisco, to the top of a hill. We're looking from very far above: at the front the shadows of unseen buildings, on our side, fall hugely and strangely across the pavement's grids and arrows. It's very early: few cars, few, ant-size pedestrians. The rising streets, too, are full of morning shadows, sharp westward spears, with eerie intense blues among them, where some shard of sunlight has ricocheted. But mostly we're looking at uninhabitable spaces: rooftops, a zebra-striped elevator bank, a blank-sided high-rise. Rest-colors: lemon, turquoise, pink, with a crisscross of what are either wires or shadows or, drifting off into pure fantasy, perspective-lines. And some of the roof-level structures have an *Arabian Nights* quality, too: a facetted dome, a spire, even what looks like a circus tent. It's Hopper: the great loneliness, the deteriorating marquee saying "Hotel" against a windowless facade. And it's Matisse: those improbable beaches on top of the city have something of his wish to offer "an easy armchair"—a shallowness enjoyed, unquestioned. The sky beyond is less vivid, almost gray.

The true innovators in painting make us see something as beautiful that has never seemed beautiful before. With Thiebaud it's the sheer clutter of the modern city, the rapidity with which things intersect with other things. The foreshortened colors of a whole on-end block, a little rainbow, in *Urban Square*. The plunging streets of San Francisco, which one feels Thiebaud might have invented, if they hadn't been given, just to have everything arrive out of nowhere and depart again as quickly. They dominate the other cityscape that's easily seen in the Bay Area, *24th Street Intersection* at the DeYoung. The little, empty intersection hangs there like Rilke's "lost carpet in the universe." None of its streets meets it on a level; the one at the rear theatrically dips, a pink-roofed bus teetering just over the edge, and then comes back up to it, out of sight. (The upper part of an apartment house shows in cliffhanger position at the far right.)

But it may be that the real dominant presence in *24th Street Intersection* is *wires*. There are so unbelievably many of them, but no more, of course, than in the everyday landscapes we take in without noticing. One veers toward the upper right-hand corner, seemingly straight off into the air. (Yes, in this age we are also wired to the sky.) Really, if you stop to figure out the perspective, it is coming down the street in our direction. Others, plunging toward the lower left, look almost underfoot. The wires do the major work—along with telephone poles and crosswalks—of squaring off that strange, empty corner. Four of them cross just above it, tiny and close together, almost a musical stave. (And the telephone poles bud out in brown boxes and insulators, making a delicate visual rhyme with four stunted, rather Japanese firs.)

That much you could get from the reproduction in the book.[1] Standing before the actual painting, you see what a playful little abstraction it also is. One of those stavelike wires is red. The phone-line boxes have red, blue, and beige in them; there are bits of red and blue in the shadows. Each sidewalk has its little colored outline. Though the realism is meticulous, the beige vacant lot is "painterly"; you can see big, sweeping brushstrokes. Smudges, that are also skid marks, show in the street. And all the brilliant areas muffled and reverberated between the twin grays of concrete and sky. "Realism," here, has the virtues and even the tricks commonly associated with abstraction; this is craftsmanship at a level where opposing schools no longer oppose.

I'll be frank; I didn't warm up to Thiebaud's early still lifes, for all their perfection of surface, until I knew the later work. Tsujimoto, however, makes some good distinctions between Thiebaud's cakes and pies and pop art—the lesser prominence of irony, less suppression of visible craft. There is even an element of personal affection—Thiebaud found pies "poetic" when he worked in restaurants as a boy.[2] But this much is clear: Thiebaud's early love of capturing surfaces, and a seemingly superficial smoothness, would serve him in good stead when he took on larger subjects where the meaning of surface was far more ambiguous. Looking at *Woman in Tub*, one of the middle period figure paintings, one sees how the seductive slickness of consumption can modulate into the slickness of depression. The bathtub is almost the whole picture, and featureless. Only the color bands of the rim, the water, and the wallpaper—indistinguishable—make it a kind of De Chirico flag, waving into emptiness. Against all this, how vivid the glaze of suntan, sweat, and strain on face and hair! But, as is often noted, it's a severed head—no visible connection to a body. And all the lines of it pull, or lapse, "downward to darkness," more clearly for all those perfect horizontals. The conscious blank of human sadness, mirrored, as always, in the unconscious blank of things. (The same quality is there, it seems to me, in those drastically abandoned accessories, *Dark Lipstick, Yellow Dress.*)

People have read the emotions of *Woman in Tub* quite differently, it's true. And often, with Thiebaud, it seems hard to tell desolation from a new key of pleasure. Which does one feel, at the whiteness through which the tiny cars glide in *Urban Freeway*? The pure blue shadows of road signs. The exaggerated, cartoonlike height and regularity of the palm trees, bigger than a nearby stadium.

Perhaps, to a painter, these would simply not be the right questions. It would all be a kind of close-in, sensuous play, whose point was that it could start with anything. A friend told me about a studio class in which the first assignment was to paint Mickey Mouse—simply to strip away all lofty, unwanted associations. But for me, being a poet, when I see something true in a new way about the surface of my world I want to learn from it about the emotions of that world. And finally—as I think Constable said—painting *is* feeling, as writing is, only under a very different code.

And so. Hopper and Matisse. Like Thiebaud, they are painters of the small details of life suspended in front of its infinite background. But that subject carries an immense gradation of possible human feelings, depending on whether the infinite is seen as the source of energy and goal of longing, or as annihilation. And so, in the conventional association, Hopper wears the mask of tragedy, Matisse that of comedy. Because with Matisse, Eros is always on the surface, Thanatos half-hidden; with Hopper, it is the other way around. Thiebaud's balance is trickier, harder to read (perhaps a contemporary's always is). Like the pop painters, he shoves our noses, for better or worse, in the bright, blank surfaces of our lives. But there is also American nostalgia, the reluctance to let go of a more textured past. In *24th Street Intersection*, the old things are done so lovingly—the thick green of the Victorian house, the two-toned car on its giddy downslant. (Nature—withdrawing, but still a measure of beauty—is also a theme: the sickly fir, with its reddish brilliance, set apart from the others.) And how does the humor fit in? Is it exuberance or black satire, when Thiebaud seems to revert to his original *metier* and thins the landscape to a cartoon? Beyond the sheer play with surface and volume, do we simply enjoy the "wrong" perspectives? (Tsujimoto has a fascinating page showing how they are right, by the conventions of Chinese and Japanese painting.)[3] Or do they add a Goyaesque scariness and vertigo? *Apartment Hill* seems almost a caricature of the Metropolitan Museum's *City on a Rock*. In several late paintings, a cerulean sky extends right down to the bottom edge on one side of the canvas, so there is no clear coming to earth. Is it a world of anxious, fake "happiness" on the edge of apocalypse? Or simply the world—the "dewdrop world," as the Buddhists say—in its unreadable evanescence, as it is, as it has always been?

However we read Thiebaud's balance, it seems clear that it could only have been attained by a West Coast painter. In the East, the heavier building materials, the age of things, their slow deliquescence, would have tipped the balance toward tragedy, as it tipped Hopper's. Thiebaud needed the lightness—in both senses, the glare of light, and the flimsiness—that makes the West not quite real to easterners, to find his own reality. *The Unbearable Lightness of Being.* I was carrying that book, as it happened, through the Oakland Museum, in the tedious breaks of jury duty, the day I stopped in front of *Urban Square*. Sabina, the woman painter in the book, ends up in California; and clearly Kundera's sense, however stereotyped, is that that destiny suits her own painting, in which every visible surface is an appearance, torn to let something else show through. And yet that expectation makes her life of restless betrayals, in its own way, tragedy . . .

Coming out of Thiebaud's world, you notice smaller things. There are the Arabian-looking tiles buried in the apartment facade, across the street from the Oakland Museum. Slightly gaudy leaves of a potted plant in the jury room dissect the complicated—but streamlined, not Gothic—windows of the public library opposite. The shallow, but live, clutter of jury duty itself—being dragged out of one's innerness onto new surfaces. (Or, on the San Francisco freeways, after the 1985 exhibition where I first saw these paintings, how many stairsteps the houses made, up how many hills.) That, to my amateur's eye, is one of the final tests of a great painter. We are where we are, more completely.

Some Tenses of Snyder

A Walk

Sunday the only day we don't work:
Mules farting around the meadow,
                    Murphy fishing.
The tent flaps in the warm
Early sun: I've eaten breakfast and I'll
                    take a walk
To Benson Lake. Packed a lunch,
Goodbye. Hopping on creekbed boulders
Up the rock throat three miles
                    Piute Creek—
In steep gorge glacier-slick rattlesnake country
Jump, land by a pool, trout skitter
The clear sky. Deer tracks.
Bad place by a falls, boulders big as houses.
Lunch tied to belt,
I stemmed up a crack and almost fell
But rolled out safe on a ledge
                    and ambled on.
Quail chicks freeze underfoot, color of stone
Then run cheep! away, hen quail fussing.
Craggy west end of Benson Lake—after edging
Past dark creek pools on a long white slope—
Lookt down in the ice-black lake
                    lined with cliff
From far above: deep shimmering trout.
A lone duck in a gunsightpass
                    steep side hill

Through slide-aspen and talus, to the east end,
Down to grass, wading a wide smooth stream
Into camp. At last.
        By the rusty three-year-
Ago left behind cookstove
Of the old trail crew,
Stoppt and swam and ate my lunch.[1]

"A Walk" is a fairly typical early Snyder poem, quiet enough to
have slipped past me three or four times before I saw into its
inner life. I found myself teaching it (for no better reason than
that it appears in a common anthology), and, wondering how to
show the students that it was more than a series of diary-jottings,
I suggested we look at verb tenses. The bewildering, unconven-
tional shifts we encountered led to a discussion of how we, in
fact, experience time.

Some time, it would seem, is past tense even while we're living it. That may be because it is lived not for its own sake but for
the sake of something in the future:

        Packed a lunch,
Goodbye.

Or it might be because we need to reassure ourselves we will survive it:

I stemmed up a crack and almost fell
But rolled out safe on a ledge
        and ambled on.

Here "I," the storyteller, splits off in alarm from the person actually struggling up the rocks. "I" is not frequent in this poem; its
only other occurrence coincides with another kind of detached
time, the time of planning, spread out like a grid over past and
future:

        I've eaten breakfast and I'll
        take a walk

As one learns more about Zen Buddhism, and Snyder's in-
volvement with it, these nuances come to seem not only not
accidental but the very core of his subject. In Zen there is a great

deal of talk about "the moment," not because longer stretches of time, and what can be accomplished in them, are unimportant, but because it is crucial not to be divided from one's own existence. In *Zen Mind, Beginner's Mind*, Shunryu Suzuki says:

> You may say, "I must do something this afternoon," but actually there is no "this afternoon." We do things one after the other. That is all. . . . To eat lunch is itself one o'clock. You will be somewhere, but that place cannot be separated from one o'clock. . . . But when we become tired of our life we may say, "I shouldn't have come to this place. It may have been much better to have gone to some other place for lunch. . . ." In your mind you create an idea of place separate from an actual time.[2]

There is a great deal of talk, too, about getting rid of the subject—not exactly because it doesn't exist, as in deconstruction, but because conscious emphasis on it is almost always defense. An "I" whose energies are completely absorbed by an object or an action does not remember that he/she is an "I." In Suzuki's words again, "When you do something, you should burn yourself completely, like a good bonfire, leaving no trace of yourself" (62). How can poetry convey this lapsing into pure attentiveness? Sometimes it comes dazedly, in the aftershock of risk and success:

> Jump, land by a pool, trout skitter,
> The clear sky.

Here we have something like a musical modulation between keys: the anxious self-addressed imperatives, the pure present, the absolute construction or verbless clause. Absolutes are common in this poem ("Deer tracks"; "deep shimmering trout"); they feel— as perhaps with all poets who use them—like little defiant rescues of pure momentariness from the grid of generalized time that is built into grammar itself. Another way might be to use a present-tense verb and interrupt it in the middle, to remind us that perception is quicker than even the simplest grammatical response:

> Then run cheep! away, hen quail fussing.

These are the extremes. Between them are many intermediate times, which escape the grammatical grid without claiming any special attunement. Present participles are a flowing activity; not wholly momentary, they do not separate out or calibrate either. Ezra Pound's mannerism, "Lookt" and "Stoppt," is also attractive, as if the elided silent syllable pushed us over some edge into immediacy. These are the poem's ordinary recourses—along with the absolute construction—when it does not want to point us too strongly in either direction.

But what, beyond temporal modes, is the poem's subject? One way to approach it might be look at what is never mentioned— the potential for fear, out among the rattlesnakes and "boulders big as houses," in the "universe of junk, all left alone" of "Bubbs Creek Haircut," where there is almost no vegetation, and the one human trace was simply abandoned, years before.[3] This fear, or metaphysical desolation, is not unfelt in the language of the poem, in "A lone duck in a gunsightpass," or even the spare glitter of "steep side hill / Through slide aspen and talus," the icy mono- chrome of "dark creek pools on a long white slope." Rather, I would argue, the desolation is continuously being disarmed by the acts of minute attention in which subject becomes one with object and can no longer fear it. This is the real process, the real underlife of the poem, which allows it to arrive with strange dig- nity at the mild self-satisfaction of "Stoppt and swam and ate my lunch."

"How does one stand / To behold the sublime," Wallace Stevens asked.[4] One of the problems for literature in the American West has always been how to deal with the sheer vastness, the prehu- man alienness, of the landscape. Is it a place of liberation for the spirit, or an emptiness that will be filled by greed and ready-made religions, or else drive mad entirely? It is at once a moral and a stylistic question. John Muir attempted to import the language of Emersonian idealism, but it didn't stick, except in second-rate travel writing. Robinson Jeffers imagined the loneliness as a Cal- vinist God, demanding sacrifice and immolation; but beyond that God waited a calm maternal Nothing, "the matrix of all shining and quieter of shining." D. H. Lawrence valued the landscape pre- cisely because it was so subversive of human purposes, and could madden—"The vast and unrelenting will of the swarming lower life, working for ever against man's attempt at a higher life."[5]

Snyder's accomplishment has been to approach the whole subject without rhetoric, taking his cue not from western writers, but from the terseness of Pound, the fact-oriented style of Williams, the calm, courtly descriptiveness of the classical Chinese masters. There is a self-annihilating love of the world in these styles through which the Western sublime can be registered, losing none of its novelty or strangeness but not causing excitation or terror. The "I" that is so mildly steadied at the end of Snyder's poem has had an experience of value, less confident than Muir's, far less darkened or troubled than Jeffers's, derived from an interchange with the land. It is an experience, again, most nearly captured in the vocabulary of Zen: the "emptiness"—Suzuki calls it "not rely[ing] on anything"—that becomes a "complete calmness" (122).

It is an odd enough history, when one thinks about it—the coolness of imagism and objectivism, nourished on cities (New York, London, Paris), meeting a body of insight from the other side of the globe and producing the first fully adequate realist poetry of the Wild West. But it is by such arcane chemistries—much more than by programs or schools—that the genuinely new in any art takes shape.

China Trade (I)

When Edmund Wilson wrote, in "The Boys in the Back Room," that the West "looks . . . out upon a wider ocean toward an Orient with which as yet any cultural communication is difficult," he begged a larger question than he was aware of broaching. When did the sense of culture we now call "Pacific Rim," in which Japan and China seem close, and not unrelated to what can be learned from the tribal cultures we have displaced, become significant in the literature of the West? This much is clear: it did not all begin with the Beat Generation. One has only to visit the unhewn-stone, but exquisitely graceful, "House of Happy Walls" that Charmian London built at Glen Ellen, after Jack London died, to see how early the Far Eastern connection could be part of a distinctly Californian high culture. A Polynesian dancing-stick provides the leitmotif for a craft-style dining room table and chairs; a Solomon Islands "King Post," frowning and conspicuously phallic, has become the newel of the upstairs stairhead.

Such a culture was congenial to the decades of anthropological work that lie behind Gary Snyder's assertion that "civilization has something to learn from the primitive."[1] (*Ishi, Last of His Tribe* is on sale, alongside Jack London's works, at the House of Happy Walls.) It was congenial, too, to the development of Western Buddhism, which, as we've seen, had its beginnings in California.

Gary Snyder is, of course, the poet who has most embodied this sense of culture for the world at large. His personal history gathers all of its elements: an undergraduate honors thesis on a Native American myth; graduate work in anthropology at Indiana University; further graduate work in Far Eastern languages, with side excursions into calligraphy, at Berkeley; eight years in

Japan as a Zen student at Daitoku-ji in Kyoto. In the 1960s, he was a preeminent spokesman for the counterculture but gave it both an ecological thrust and a Far Eastern humor it lacked in other hands. While others romanticized guns, he led sitting meditation outside the fence of the Oakland Army Terminal. Now, late in life, he has become the most articulate proponent of the idea that the West Coast has evolved its own culture, distinct from the Euro-American, out of precisely this combination of sources.

My concern here is not so much Snyder's cultural work (which in any case has been discussed exhaustively by others) as what he has brought over into English from the unique forms and attitudes of Far Eastern poetry. Crispness of form in the short lyric—the imagist lessons Pound had already learned in his own work with Chinese poetry—are part, but not all, of the story. Stephen Owen, in his great study *Traditional Chinese Poetry and Poetics: Omen of the World* (a book Snyder recommends enthusiastically), emphasizes the everydayness of Chinese poetry, its "occasional" character. Chinese "poetic theory . . . grounded a poem in the moment, in a particular place, and often in address to a particular person."[2] Owen contrasts (not to its advantage) the Western lyric "I," which, he argues, is already somewhat depersonalized and grandiose because it is addressed to the unknown reader who can confer "greatness." More specific in its names and places than the Western lyric has been until recently, the Chinese lyric nevertheless does not display the wish that the poet should be different from other people, less mortal.

This is because Chinese particularity is grounded in the Buddhist sense of impermanence. Everything is temporary, the greatest as well as the smallest things; we are not in control of the world; and the things we think give our lives significance and hope are also evanescent. And yet, Buddhism also offers a strange kind of rescue from the potential despair of that perspective, by a sudden immersion in the moment, in which distinctions between subject and object vanish, and with them fear and desire. Classical Chinese poetry is full of these strange, sudden rescuers. T'ao Yuan-ming, feeling "myself decay with time's passing," looks up and says, "My old home is there on the southern mountain." Su Tung-p'o, grieving at the vanishing of the past, is suddenly transported back into it, by his memory of "our lame donkeys braying."[3] In such moments we are put into another time and space, outside the realm of "significance," the place of Buddha in meditation, who, as Rilke put it in *New Poems*, "forgets what we experience / and experiences what turns us away."[4]

Rilke notwithstanding, these are not the characteristic assumptions of the Western lyric tradition. Our more individualistic sense of where value lies makes our lament for its passing, our desire to preserve it, more passionate and specific: the unique beloved, the one defining childhood day. Here, the Western lyric "I"—*pace* Stephen Owen, who contends it is always more of a fiction than its Chinese counterpart, being addressed to eternity—may in fact be more personal because of this passionate clinging. Our sharpened sense of the individual is nothing to regret, for it gives a special acuteness to our love of the world. But our obsession with immortality may make us fail to notice, or merely regret and romanticize, those who have fallen through the net of heroic individuation. Such a figure as dominates Snyder's early poem "Hay for the Horses":[5]

He had driven half the night
From far down San Joaquin
Through Mariposa, up the
Dangerous mountain roads,
And pulled in at eight a.m.
With his big truckload of hay
   behind the barn.
With winch and ropes and hooks
We stacked the bales up clean
To splintery redwood rafters
High in the dark, flecks of alfalfa
Whirling through shingle-cracks of light,
Itch of haydust in the
   sweaty shirt and shoes.
At lunchtime under Black oak
Out in the old corral,
—The old mare nosing lunchpails,
Grasshoppers crackling in the weeds—
"I'm sixty-eight," he said,
"I first bucked hay when I was seventeen.

I thought, that day I started,
I sure would hate to do this all my life.
And dammit, that's just what
I've gone and done."

The sense of anonymity, of lost chances, a life gone without choice—the commonest human fate—would be heartbreaking, if it weren't so immediately turned into humor, and thus mastered, by the victim himself. And there is another kind of mastery hidden in the sonata structure of the poem, marked off by the indented lines: theme A (the old man), then theme B, then theme A again. But what is theme B? It is the world of work, in which for the moment one loses sight of more abstract concerns. But surely it is also a "clean"-ness and mystery in the material world itself, a flickery yet immense precision, "flecks of alfalfa / Whirling" like galaxies through light and dark. It is what, like Proust's madeleine, or Su Shih's lame donkey, has the power to bring the past back entire. It fuses subject and object, until our serving such a world ("Hay for the Horses") no longer has any quality of pathos, of loss of self. Humor as a strategy of rescue is familiar to the Western lyric; but this other kind of rescue, it seems to me, is the uniquely Far Eastern resonance that Snyder has captured and domesticated, nuance by nuance, into the American language, in his poetry.

Eastern aesthetics, as I've suggested, has a different sense of the relation of the local to the universal than Western. Everything vanishes; everything has Buddha nature—so that wherever you dip into the stream, you are in touch with the whole. If there is no tendency, as in Western poetry, to aggrandize the personal, there is no need to apologize for dwelling on the insignificant or for merely noticing. If the short occasional lyric is one consequence of such an aesthetic, another is the vast unending scroll-paintings, full of incident but utterly without hierarchies of importance, that have given their name to Snyder's long poem, forty years in the making: *Mountains and Rivers without End*.

From the poem's opening lines, we see how the painting's two elements—water, which is constantly changing; rock, which seems never to—stand for the paradoxical union of steadiness and change that is the mind's in meditation, the artist's in the "created space":

Clearing the mind and sliding in
    to that created space,
a web of waters streaming over rocks[6]

And we see how the poem will follow that meditative mind, being
on the one hand very concrete and local, on the other utterly unpredictable as to where it will go next, since it is always aware of
impermanence and boundlessness. Calligraphy—with its resem-
blance to action painting, since the stroke, once made, cannot be
taken back—is another metaphor for this method. Shamanic pos-
session, lending one's voice to whatever voice comes, is a third.

Old ghost ranges, sunken rivers, come again
    stand by the wall and tell their tale,
walk the path, sit the rains,
grind the ink, wet the brush, unroll the
    broad white space

So, a poem of journeys: the many literal journeys of the poet's
adventurous life; nightmare journeys in which a companion says,
"Now we have come to / where we die"; historical journeys, like
that of Hsuan Tsang, who carried the elements of Buddhism from
India to China on his back. Yet all the journeys seem in some sense
oscillations between the two elements of the scroll, or of "Hay for
the Horses." In "Night Highway 99," for example, we find *dukka*,
the Buddhist sense of universal suffering and impermanence—

"I had a girl in Oakland who worked
for a doctor, she was a nurse, she let him
eat her. She died of tuberculosis
& I drove back that night to Portland
nonstop, crying all the way"

—closely juxtaposed with the rescuing power of the utterly
quirky, efficient, momentary:

"I picked up an Italian tree surgeon
in Port Angeles once, he had all his
saws and tools all screwed & bolted on
a beat-up bike."

115

Scholars are, I am sure, already at work elucidating the hidden elements of structure, repeated motifs, Joycean overarching myth, and progression in *Mountains and Rivers*.[7] If I emphasize instead its quality as an all-inclusive method, a world-plenitude kept interesting, even irresistible, by a characteristic way of seeing, it's not out of any disrespect for Snyder the conscious maker. I suspect that many of the modern long poems, despite their ingenious pretenses to structure, really convince not as stories or arguments but as similar world-plenitudes. It's the primary thing that draws me back to *The Bridge* and *Paterson*, works whose structures I have labored over exegetically. It's the only way I now read Pound's *Cantos*, whose ideas about history and philosophy are less congenial to me.

Some readers have felt that Snyder's best work since *Turtle Island* has been in prose—the poems too often mere underlinings of points already made. *Mountains and Rivers* should win them back. All the old themes are there—the value of the tribal, wilderness, the possibility of new locally based cultures as an alternative to "globalization" (though there is enough imaginative room for a section regarding New York City as an ecosystem, the "Sea of Information"). But the familiar themes seem, now, a circumambient atmosphere around the local acts of seeing, like Pound's Mediterranean light. There is very little prosy or didactic insistence.

But there is one thematic element that seems to me radically new in *Mountains and Rivers*, compared with earlier Snyder. One might call it the eros of geology. The poet who once wrote "No one loves rock, but we are here,"[8] now attempts—on a scale unprecedented even in Jeffers—to invite "Old ghost ranges, sunken rivers" to inhabit his voice and "tell their tale." The language of geology, and related sciences, lends the poem much of its local energy, revitalizing the condensed style, the ambiguous noun-verb clusters, of Snyder's early work: "glacier-flour and outwash gravel fan down from the hills." Or:

amber river waters
dark from muskeg acids, irons,
murk the stream of tide-wall eagre coming up
over the sandspit   ("Haida Gwai North Coast")

Such description can overlap with descriptions of language itself—for Snyder, *pace* the Saussureans, always an accretion of our experience in the world. And both can overlap with religious vision. So the irrigation system of Ladakh, channeling "Water from the ice-fields," becomes "'The long wide tongue of the Buddha' led into asides."

Geology overlaps, also, with erotic experience. The sense, grounded in Buddhism, of connection not only with other sentient beings but with the inanimate blossoms out here in a kind of landscape-eros. The most neutral, eons-long process seems imbued with the sense of a lurking mother- or lover-figure. "Mother / Earth / loves to love," Snyder writes, and he means it. In the section I have mainly been quoting from, "An Offering for Tara," the geological lines

> Rock stuff always folding
> turned back again, re-folded,
> wrapping, twisting in and out like dough

—already carried across boundaries of the nourishing and the unnourishing by the simile of "dough"—are juxtaposed with this quote from a love poem:

> "Black as bees are the plaits of your hair"

Finally, in the "Rivermouth" section of "The Flowing," there is a sexual consummation between man and the inanimate that might surprise even Whitman:

> —O pressing song
>   liquid butts and nibbles
>   between the fingers—in the thigh—
>   against the eye
>
>   .   .   .   .   .   .
>
> The root of me
> hardens and lifts to you,
> thick flowing river,
>   my skin shivers. I quit
>
> making this poem.

But the presumption implicit in such assertions of oneness with the inanimate will be severely, and dramatically, tested in the poem's climactic section, "The Mountain Spirit." As Snyder has freely acknowledged, the section retells a Japanese Noh play, *Yamamba*, in which a dancer famous for her impersonation of the Mountain Spirit goes on a pilgrimage through the mountains and encounters the Spirit herself, who asks to see the dance. The parallels to the Japanese text are in fact quite minute, much closer than a naïve reader would ever imagine; but Snyder has managed a thoroughly American transmutation.

> The North American way to tell the story goes thus:
> Throughout Western North America there are tales of the Mountain Spirits—sometimes fierce and jagged as lightning, sometimes smooth and sweet as a rainbow, sometimes seen as an old ragged woman. Some years back, in San Francisco, there was a poet who made his reputation largely on the basis of a poem he had written about the Mountain Spirit, even though he had not actually visited the mountains very much himself.
>   One year he decided to pay a visit to the unique groves of ancient bristlecone pines—the oldest living beings in the world.[9]

The testing that the "poet," Snyder's more naïve surrogate, must undergo is extreme. And the poem manufactured for the occasion, "The Mountain Spirit," is also extreme—an effort to make poetry speak pure geology, speak from the point of view of the inanimate, of nonhuman time. ("For a creature to speak of all that scale of time—what for?" the Mountain Spirit asks.) We do not quite know how much it pleases the Mountain Spirit, but she and the poet end up "danc[ing] the pine tree"—appropriately enough, since the tiny live portion of the bristlecone grows on the dead part, "four thousand years of mineral glimmer," as the poet has attempt to live off of the deadest, oldest portion of the cosmos he can experience.

The only moral the Mountain Spirit draws explicitly is "All art and song / is sacred to the real. / As such." It follows closely on a response in the Japanese play, but it draws distinctions that have always been important to Snyder. "*All* art"—that is, we are not concerned with distinctions between high and low genres, masters and primitives. "Sacred to the real"—that is, no play of "signifiers" without a "signified," though the relation of the two is no simple correspondence but the hopeful gesture ritual action casts across a void. "As such"—how we complicate things, simple if imponderable in themselves!

But for me the true moral comes a few pages later, in the quote from Milarepa with which the poet responds to his first glimpse of the Black Rock desert, "silvery flats that curved over the edge." (It is also one of the epigraphs to the entire poem.)

O, ah! The
awareness of emptiness
brings forth a heart of compassion!

This is, in fact, a statement I first heard Snyder quote, with great passion, in a discussion at Tor House about Jeffers's association of western loneliness with nightmare, tragedy, and nihilistic transcendence. And it expresses an attitude, new in literature, toward the American West and the experiences of space, time, matter, it imposes on us. Landscape becomes the object, and the teacher, of "compassion." Feeling unbounded and exposed, one values the present moment more, in oneself and in others. One way to look at *Mountains and Rivers* is as the great and necessary counterstatement to Jeffers, the Mahayana to his Hinayana, from a writer finally at home in the West. (Snyder once, in a class lecture, described Jeffers as a Hinayana *arhat*, one of the early Buddhist holy men who, after attaining Enlightenment, fled the world in order not to be contaminated.) Now, at the centerless center that loneliness cannot drive mad—"No flatness because no not-flatness"—the poet and his lover, "leg hard-twined to leg," look out serenely at "[t]he tooth / of a far peak called King Lear."

*   *   *   *

I had the great privilege of hearing Snyder read *Mountains and Rivers* in its entirety, the evening of August 11, 2000, at the North Columbia Schoolhouse Cultural Center, near Snyder's home in the high foothills of Nevada County. The reading began at 7:30, and lasted, with three intermissions, until past two in the morning. We walked down behind the Cultural Center (an actual

one-room schoolhouse until 1979) to a small outdoor amphitheater. A long sunset rayed through ponderosa trunks behind
the stage, as the three local musicians who were to accompany
Snyder warmed up. One more pine, painted on a screen—the sole
prop of Japanese Noh drama, also the bristlecone of "The Mountain Spirit"—occupied center stage. On benches and blankets, in
the growing coolness, spectators—a few from far away, but mostly
Snyder's San Juan Ridge neighbors—passed around food and
wine. It was for all the world like a school picnic, or one of those
twilight gatherings to hear a ranger's talk in a National Park.
Children dozed off; stars appeared.

A conch shell—the morning wake-up call in Zen monaster-
ies—signaled the beginning of the performance, and would be
repeated after each intermission. Snyder was in top form, as he
would remain throughout, except for a slight asthmatic tightness
in the wee hours. Indeed, it was the most quietly, *seriously* ex-
pressive reading I've ever heard him give, perhaps because he was
free to take his audience's welcome for granted, and attend only
to the text. The musicians behind him scrambled to change instruments in a kind of global jam session, veering from wailing
American blues for the *On the Road* mood of "Night Highway
Ninety-Nine," to Balinese gamelan instruments in the Asian sections, to the earth-and-pebble music of the Australian didgeridoo.
For all the homemade feeling, I couldn't help thinking of Yeats:

> I have prepared my peace
> With learned Italian things,
> And the proud stones of Greece,
> Poet's imaginings . . .

With Snyder, of course, the terms would have to be different: it
would be tribal things, the not-so-proud stones of Himalayan
gompas. And the "memories" in *Mountains and Rivers* are less
of the "words of women" than of places (or place-women), ones
few Caucasians of Snyder's level of education would ever have
seen. Yet a "peace" had been prepared, no less carefully and mag-
isterially than Yeats's. And the crowd in front of him was not only
its audience but an integral part of it. Most people stayed to the
end, though they huddled in blankets and sleeping bags against
the night coldness. One spectator picked up one of Snyder's chants

and continued it, until the gentle, tacit judgment of the crowd persuaded him to stop.

It was an image of civility conjoined with freedom, the same image, really, put forth in the last section of *Mountains and Rivers* itself: the group camping trip on the playa in the Black Rock Desert, the prehistoric lake bed so flat and uninterrupted the kids can safely ride their bikes in "great arcs . . . in darkness" with "no lights—just planet Venus glinting / by the calyx crescent moon." Later, noticing how the grasshoppers "all somehow swarm down here," the campers roast them, "sons and daughters in the circle / eating grasshoppers grimacing."

A Taoist civility, local enough, ingenious enough in living off the land, that it does not need to regard life as a state of war, does not need the rules—for bicycle traffic, for instance—that more crowded, regimented social orders must impose. It stands against, not only the spread of homogeneous shopping strips, globalization, media-derived culture, but also against the conservative belief that only a highly organized culture can preserve civility, that the loosening of rules we call the '60s could only end in the chaos of Altamont and Manson. This Hobbesian view is refuted by an oddly Lockean faith in a basic human reasonableness and flexibility, attainable through the reinvention of small communities. The one major literary prize that explicitly considered *Mountains and Rivers* in the year of its publication, I am told, called it "good but dated." On San Juan Ridge that night, it didn't seem dated at all. It seemed likely, in some version of its implications, to outlast most of the things contemporary America finds interesting—if anything human, or civil, outlasts them.

Aristotle in Montana

not "tragedy"
in the sense of newspapers
—Robert Pinsky

Tragedy means to die . . .
—Robert Lowell

Science and scientific fact, as we have seen, bulk large in the
western writer's sense of our place in the universe. Still, I was surprised and intrigued to find Norman Maclean, in his last great
book, *Young Men and Fire,* insisting on the word "tragedy" in
approaching the deaths of thirteen young Smokejumpers in a forest fire in 1949. For such natural disasters, as Pinsky or any high
school teacher could tell you, are "tragedy" only "in the sense of
newspapers." Real tragedy is a moral matter: a complex though
admirable hero is brought down by his "tragic flaw," thus demon-
strating the "order of the universe." And Maclean, of all people,
should have known that.

Let me explain. Norman Maclean was a colleague of my
father's at the University of Chicago; I knew him slightly when I
was growing up. I knew that he came from Montana, and that his
family went back there every summer—which seemed an exotic
choice to me then, even in comparison to my own family's divided
East/West lives.

I knew, too, that Norman Maclean was one of the Chicago
Aristotelians, famous for insisting on the importance of Aristotle's *Poetics* in understanding literary structure, even in the
twentieth century. The Aristotelians emphasized what one might
call the journeyman aspects of art—plot construction, suspense,

control over the reader's expectations, "unity," and pacing. They agreed with their master that plot was more important than character, and undertook to correct both the New Critics' delight in verbal texture and the symbol-hunters' search for archetypal or philosophical depth. As a young man, I bristled at what seemed to me a triumphant reductiveness in all of this—the village explainer showing that, as in Oz, there is only a wizened, if clever, little man behind all of the smoke and mirrors. The Aristotelians were the last group, among my father's colleagues, whom I would have expected to produce a great imaginative writer.

And yet, in the years when he advocated Aristotle in the classroom and published famously little criticism, Maclean was preparing himself to be exactly that. When I found myself going back to one of those famously few essays, "Episode, Scene, Speech, and Word: The Madness of Lear," it was partly to understand how his critical mind related to his imaginative mind; but more specifically to understand how he conceived of "tragedy," and how that conception shaped his own idiosyncratic venture into the genre. What was Maclean doing? Was he subtilizing our understanding of Aristotle beyond the reach of the high school teacher? Or was he redefining the term itself, for that western landscape where our significant encounters are less with our fellow humans than with physical immensity, physical force?

A little of both, I suspect. The word for "tragic flaw," in Aristotle, is more accurately translated "error or frailty," and in any case receives less emphasis than the "change of fortune . . . from good to bad."[1] Already in the Lear essay, Maclean is suggesting that while some tragedies are exclusively tragedies of character, others are not: "Othello's fate was his own—at least many of us could have escaped it; but Lear's tragedy comes to a point where it threatens what we should wish to be with inevitable inclusion."[2] And the latter kind is perhaps the deepest of all, since it reflects on the value of existence: "the question of whether the universe is something like what Lear hoped it was or very close to what he feared it was, is still, tragically, the current question" (100).

The Mann Gulch fire, if it is tragedy at all, is surely the kind that "threatens what we should wish to be with inevitable inclusion." The Smokejumpers' mistakes are at worst "errors," not flaws. If they are tragic heroes, it is because Maclean sees being a tough woodsman as a metaphysical vocation, in a way that would surely never have occurred to him if he had been a professor alone or a woodsman alone, not both. "It is very important to a lot of people to make unmistakably clear to themselves and to the universe that they love the universe but are not intimidated by it and will not be shaken by it, no matter what it has in store. Moreover, they demand something from themselves early in life that can be taken ever after as demonstration of this abiding feeling."[3]

If the Smokejumpers have "hubris," overweening ambition— a term, again, more prominent in high school discussions than it is in Aristotle—it is because they are convinced it is possible to win; that the "universe" may not be, in part, what Lear fears it is. Literally "young men who came from the sky," "They were still so young they hadn't learned to count the odds and to sense they might owe the universe a tragedy" (299, 19).

"In a modern tragedy," Maclean cautions us, "you have to watch out for little details rather than big flaws" (56). So perhaps the meaning of "tragedy" will be stretched a little, after all, for the pragmatic, unforgiving world west of the Mississippi. "Past tragedy," he tells us, "refrained from speaking of its association with screwups and blowups" (92)—"screwups" of course being practical rather than moral errors, "blowups" the technical term for the freak explosion of a forest fire at the heart of the Mann Gulch story.

Still, there must be an artistic difference between "catastrophe" and "tragedy"; and that difference for Maclean, as a true Aristotelian, lies in the discovery of "shape, form, pattern" in a "universe" that seems "composed of catastrophes and missing parts."

> [A]nyone coming down the Gates of the Mountains can
> see that the laminations of ocean beds compressed in the
> cliffs on one side of the river match the laminations in the
> opposite cliffs, and, looking up, can see that an arch, now
> disappeared into sky, originally joined both cliffs. There
> are also missing parts to the story of the lonely crosses
> ahead of us. . . . What if, by searching the earth and even
> the sky for these missing parts, we should find enough of

them to see catastrophe change into the shape of remembered tragedy? (46)

Scientific and factual knowledge, one should note, may play as much of a role in this tragic "shape" as artistic empathy. (The geology of the Gates of the Mountains *does* have a real, though hidden, connection to what went wrong.) Both kinds of knowledge, it seems, enter into Maclean's special sense of Aristotelian tragic "purgation"—"the part of me and the tragedy that knows more about forests and fires because of this forest fire," so that, "[i]f now the dead of the fire should awaken and I should be stopped beside a cross, I would no longer be nervous if asked the first and last question of life, How did it happen?" (87)

Still, "shape"—Aristotle's "unity of action"—has to be created artistically, not simply discovered. Maclean may hope "that at times life takes on the shape of art and that the remembered remnants of those moments are largely what we come to mean by life." But there is always the danger, especially in the "true" stories we call creative nonfiction, that things will fail to "fit together dramatically," whether because of unsolved factual mysteries, or the reticences and amnesias of "frightened people" (144). This danger too reflects back on "what we come to mean by life": "there's a lot of tragedy in the universe that has missing parts and comes to no conclusion, including probably the tragedy that awaits you and me" (156).

There is a further difficulty. In the Lear essay, Maclean writes, "expository as well as imaginative writing should not be merely what the reader expected it to be—or why should it be written or read?—and the unexpected should not be immediately and totally announced . . . for, if the whole is immediately known, why should the writer or reader proceed farther?" (95). In the case of Mann Gulch, we know the important outcomes from the start: a fire blew up, thirteen men died, three escaped, in ways and for reasons that are generally clear. How much suspense can the small "missing parts" add? How will Maclean persuade us to "proceed farther"? In answering these questions, we will come near the core not only of the subtlety of Maclean's art but of its profound humaneness.

*   *   *   *

Lear had been a successful king and Shakespeare had written great tragedies, but neither had ventured far into madness.

This was a lonely moment in art.

We propose to follow Lear and Shakespeare across the heath to the fields of Dover on what for both was a unique experience. . . . [O]ur problems will be some of those that were Shakespeare's, because he was attending Lear and at the same time was on his way toward a consummation in the art of tragic writing. ("Lear," 97–98)

Most literary criticism makes a choice at the very start, by a kind of Heisenbergian uncertainty principle. Either it focuses on the artist as maker—as the Chicago Aristotelians often did—to the exclusion of granting the characters reality; or else it treats the fictive world as if it were the real world, ignoring the fact that that world comes into being, literally, conscious choice by conscious choice. It is Maclean's peculiar generosity as a critic that he refuses this either/or, and thereby arrives at the odd but poignant conception of author and character as journeymates, companions.

This conception, as we shall see, underwrites the whole method of *Young Men and Fire.* "A storyteller, unlike a historian," Maclean writes, "must follow compassion wherever it leads him. He must be able to accompany his characters, even into smoke and fire, and bear witness to what they thought and felt even when they themselves no longer knew" (102). The word "lonely," from the "Lear" essay, reverberates through *Young Men and Fire:* "the lonely crosses ahead of us" (46), "Heat and loneliness were becoming the only remaining properties" (297), and, in the book's last words, "my wife on her brave and lonely way to death" (301). So too does the "Lear" essay's metaphor of the journey, the author "*walk[ing]* the final distance" with his characters (102; italics mine). His journey, like theirs, will use his utmost capacities, "everything I know and feel." And like theirs, it may fail. But it is the only way, finally, to appease loneliness, to establish "the outer limit of friendship with the dead" (223).

*   *   *   *

Maclean will fulfill his promise to accompany the dead through their final moments; but what of the intervening pages? "Shakespeare," he tells us, "had his own set of dismaying problems—the problem of objectifying tragic thoughts and feelings into commensurate actions and then of dividing these actions into parts which would be themselves little tragedies and yet stations on the road to some more ultimate suffering" ("Lear," 102). These stages—as Aristotle would emphasize—must be "actions," not mere soliloquies or reflections. They must, in Eliot's phrase, be "objective correlatives." They are "complex variations" on the central tragic theme—in Lear's case, madness—and are accomplished by doublings or mirrorings: "a noble man going mad, accompanied by a character professionally not 'normal,' meeting a character whose life depends on his appearing mad, amid a storm such as makes everyone believe that the universe and even the gods are not stable" (104). And there seems a special magic to the number three. As there are three parallel characters, "[t]hree scenes lead to the madness of Lear and are alternated with three leading to the blinding of Gloucester" (103). Even in the essay itself, "[t]he third time that we shall consider Lear upon the Heath will be the last, for the full art of tragedy has three dimensions, like anything with depth" (107).

In *Young Men and Fire*, Maclean too prolongs his action through "little tragedies" by giving the Smokejumpers, like Lear, two primary doubles, along with a few archetypal ones (General Custer, Christ).[4] Part 1 of the book ends with another death in Mann Gulch, that of the scientist Harry Gisborne. Gisborne, "the man above all others who made the study of fire a science, was determined to examine Mann Gulch firsthand before winter came and destroyed crucial evidence. . . . So despite a severe heart ailment he was determined to make the trip. . . . Almost literally he was to die for his theory about the cause of the Mann Gulch fire" (124).

Gisborne is a tragic double for the Smokejumpers not only because he loses his life, but because in the process he must despair of the value of his highest definition of himself, his theory. Halfway through the walk in the Mann Gulch he is convinced that no firewhirl occurred; later, he is forced to acknowledge that one did, but not in the way he would have predicted. Because his companion, Jansson, happened to record by numbers "points where the two had stopped to talk," Maclean is able to absorb Gisborne's disillusionment and, of course, his death, into the dominant metaphor for the Smokejumpers' last race: "By now the rest stops were becoming stations of the cross" (138). (An especially alert reader might notice that the word "stations" is already present in Maclean's account of the subordinate tragedies in *King Lear*.)

Gisborne is a hero to Maclean particularly because he accepts his own error not only ungrudgingly but almost with enthusiasm. "To Gisborne, science started and ended in observation, and theory should always be endangered by it. . . . For a scientist, this is a good way to live and die, maybe the ideal way for any of us— excitedly finding we were wrong and excitedly waiting for tomorrow to come so that we can start over" (137, 139).

With Gisborne's death, "tragedy" takes on an intellectual as well as a physical dimension. Intellectual work, too, can be something that requires unqualified commitment, although, or because, it may cost one everything. Artistic work cannot be far behind, and has, necessarily, the same "ideal way." Will Norman Maclean come out of Mann Gulch alive? How many cherished hypotheses will he have to discard? Where will the artistic shape he makes of them rank on the Aristotelian *gradus* of "magnitude" he sets forth so uncompromisingly in the "Lear" essay?[5] (This last question may remain, tragically, unanswered. Maclean did not finish revising *Young Men and Fire;* he abandoned it when he became too ill. The anecdotal evidence is that he died satisfied with parts of the book, but not with the whole.)[6]

Maclean makes himself the third in the magic triad of risk-takers with considerable finesse and tact. First, Maclean—or his editors—have chosen to begin the book with "Black Ghost," a story involving a close call Maclean survived as a young firefighter, so that, indeed, the Smokejumpers are "young men whose lives I might have lived" (300). On page 166, Maclean introduces the idea of a "kiss of death" touching all those involved in a "first-class catastrophe." Only four pages later, we learn that Maclean himself, like Gisborne, has a heart problem, and that *his* companions, too, have tried to dissuade him from returning to the Gulch. In standing up to them, he invokes, for the first time, his wife's "brave and lonely way to death," reminding his companions that her ashes are scattered on "a mountain downriver no farther than twelve miles from here," and that "[n]obody should feel bad if I should remain behind on one of these hills that looks her way" (170).

With each of these redoublings (Gisborne, Maclean, Maclean's wife), the Smokejumpers' fate becomes more an image of universal human fate, closer to Robert Lowell's "Tragedy means to die." And for this reason, it becomes more worthy of the most sweeping, riskiest parallel, "[t]he Christian scene of suffering, where hill meets sky" (174)—a parallel, as we shall see, that grows more and more prominent as the book comes to a close.

Of course, we are pretty sure that Norman Maclean will not die before the book is over. Yet his last journey to Mann Gulch threatens him with enough of the Smokejumpers' fate, as well as Gisborne's, to be the crucial ordeal that will enable to him to keep his promise and relive their last moments. The heat, "[b]etween 120 and 130 degrees" in the bottom of the Gulch, just short of the "lethal" 140 (196), teaches him "how it might feel to die in the heat of the Inferno." On the "76 percent slope," he also "ha[s] to learn how to die in the Inferno always falling down, and always falling down I now know is a terrible way to die—it destroys the confidence before it destroys the body, and it must be terrible to die with nothing left but the body" (205). Finally, Maclean must also share the Smokejumpers' fear of mental loss of control ("I was more and more afraid I could not think when I needed to" [201]), as well as Gisborne's fear of seeing a life's work come to nothing. Yet, in the event, it is this trip that ends in the discovery of the last "missing parts," Dodge's wooden cross and Sallee and Rumsey's tree, that confirm the correct interpretation; so that, with great elegance, intellectual inquiry and emotional reenactment are brought to rest in the same instant. At this moment, it seems to me, whatever cavils one may have about redundancy or posthumous rearrangement, the *structural* arc of the book is complete. "I was no longer sorry for us. Such can be the effect of the beauty of a very short poem" (208).

*   *   *   *

One question remains to be explored before we come to the final journey: a question of style. In the "Lear" essay, Maclean writes:

"There are moments . . . which have a size that is unmentionable, moments which cannot, at least at the instant, be fully faced or exactly spoken of by those who must endure them. Poetry may make a perfection out of what would be an error in exposition, and moments such as these may set at naught the rule of composition teachers that "such," "it," and "this" should not be used without a definite, grammatical antecedent" (113). The Mann Gulch fire, like Lear's madness, has a "size that is unmentionable," that threatens consciousness itself. "[V]iewing total conflagration is literally blinding. . . . Pictures, then, of a big fire are pictures of many realities, designed so they change into each other and fit ultimately into a single picture of one monster becoming another monster" (*Young Men and Fire*, 293). So it should not surprise us that all approaches to direct description of the fire involve a violation of literary rules. When Jansson narrowly escapes being trapped himself, the "spot fires" ahead of the main fire are described as "flower[s]" and "bouquets." Then, when the blowup begins, "the flowers that had grown into a garden distended themselves into an enormous light bulb and a great mixed metaphor. Flowers and light bulbs don't seem to mix, but the light bulb of the mind strung itself inside with flame and flowers, bloated and rounded itself at its top with gases, then swirled upgulch" (85–86).

Maclean points out his own violation with his characteristic humor—"so openly mischievous and yet deadpan," Richard Wertime has called it—yet the joke is serious.[7] Human cognition fails in the face of apocalyptic and instantaneous change; and what is metaphoric coherence but a little illustration of cognitive power?

When Maclean himself gets his glimpse of the fire, in its last stages, "[i]t was a world of still-warm ashes that had incubated once-hot poles. The black poles looked as if they had been born of the gray ashes as the result of some vast effort at sexual intercourse on the edges of the afterlife" (11). The almost inept, monstrous sexuality of this passage is harder to accept than the "mixed metaphor" later. (Though it helps to remember that Maclean has associated "catastrophe" with the "id," and that the world Lear fears is one where "sex and self are the sole laws of life" ["Lear," 100].) But I suspect Maclean wants to make us uncomfortable, and so show us how hard it is, on the edge of primal chaos, to distinguish the creative from the destructive, the impressive from the obscene. This becomes the point, certainly, in the vast symphony of mixed metaphors, "fire . . . procreating its meanings" in "bi-visual" or "tri-visual" forms, by which Maclean tries to reproduce the Smokejumpers' experience of the fire just before smoke cut off the visual entirely. The "spot-fires" become "poisonous little mushrooms," which then "bred instantly . . . into a vast bulbous head with a giant stalk." "[S]ometimes [it] looked like a bulbous mushroom impregnated by a snake in the grass and sometimes like gray brains boiling out of the crevice of the earth. Then the brains themselves became bi-visual and changed again into suffering gray intestines" (294–95).

The "mushroom" metaphor is no more fortuitous than the proverbial, and Edenic, snake. In the very next paragraph, Maclean describes Henry Moore's statue commemorating the first nuclear chain reaction at the University of Chicago, "intentionally bi-visual from every point of view. Wherever you stand, the bronze looks like both an atomic mushroom and a skull, and is meant to." With our new mastery, we have a new image of "the explosive power of the universe." It is at once cosmically creative, a kind of Big Mind, like the "brains" that will boil even out of the burning ground, and a new Triumph of Death. "Perhaps it could see all of us," Maclean adds, grimly (295). If the smoke cloud from the Mann Gulch blowup looked, as Maclean says, a little like the atomic mushroom, it too raises a version of Lear's question that is "still, tragically, current."

* * * *

The most difficult question, in Aristotle, is what tragedy does for us; why we get *pleasure*—a crucial matter for him, as for his followers at Chicago—from the depiction of terrible things. "[T]hrough pity and fear effecting the proper purgation of these emotions," goes the famous phrase, the most controversial in the *Poetics*, not least because, as Francis Ferguson explains, here too the obscene and the impressive are not far apart: "[t]he Greek word ["catharsis"] can mean either the cleansing of the body (a medical term) or the cleansing of the spirit (a religious term). Some interpreters are shocked by it, because they do not wish to associate poetry with laxatives and enemas; others insist that Aristotle had the religious meaning in mind."[8]

Maclean gives tragic purgation many meanings, including, as we have seen, scientific explanation. But his radical innovation—in keeping with his concept of companionship in his criticism—is not clearly to distinguish the purgation experienced by author, characters, and audience. When "fear and pity" enter, they are experienced first and foremost by the Smokejumpers themselves. In their final thoughts, which, Maclean severely reminds us, probably did not have "much size to them" (298), fear came first. With the loss of "structure" and cognition, their "loneliness" was "like a great jump backwards into the sky" (297). But since their death "was not . . . for most of them, a terrible death" (they suffocated, before they were burned), Maclean conjectures that fear was not their last thought. It was "burned away," not only by the heat but—as in our literary experience—by "the end of tragedy" itself. Pity outlives fear, as it does in Ferguson's reading of Aristotle.[9] "The pity that remains is perhaps the last and only emotion felt if it is the young and unfulfilled who suffer the tragedy. It is pity in the form of self-pity, but the compassion felt for themselves by the tragic young is self-pity transformed into some divine bewilderment, one of the few emotions in which the young and the universe are the only characters." This "divine bewilderment" finds its "most eloquent expression" in Christ's words on the Cross, "My God, my God, why hast thou forsaken me?" (299).

But, Maclean cautions, the "universe" will not answer. "[D]ivine bewilderment" has to "find its answer, if at all, in its own final act." And this, Maclean believes, the Smokejumpers did, purging pity in themselves so that it can be purged in all of us:

> Dr. Hawkins, the physician who went in with the rescue crew the night the men were burned, told me that, after the bodies had fallen, most of them had risen again, taken a few steps, and fallen again, this final time like pilgrims in prayer, facing the top of the hill, which on that slope is nearly east. . . .
>
> The evidence, then, is that at the very end beyond thought and beyond fear and beyond even self-compassion and divine bewilderment there remains some firm intention to continue doing forever and ever what we last hoped to do on earth. (300)

We might remember, here, Maclean's own words, at the moment his intellectual and artistic problems are solved: "I was no longer sorry for us" (208). "[F]irm intention" ("Crying *What I do is me: for that I came,*" as Gerard Manley Hopkins wrote, in a very different context) not only transcends pity and fear, it comes "as close as body and spirit can to establishing a unity of themselves with earth, fire, and perhaps the sky" (300).

One would hesitate a long time, and rightly, before calling Maclean a mystical writer. Yet his sense that opposing the universe (in the sense of "making unmistakably clear to [it] . . . that they love [it] but are not intimidated by it") leads ultimately to a "unity" with the universe picks up one of the oldest themes in the literature of the American West. It is the feeling most incomprehensible and repellent to Yvor Winters's rational pessimism. But it is quite in accord with Jeffers and Steinbeck, with Gary Snyder's brand of Buddhism, most of all, perhaps, with the "oldest religion" of Lawrence's New Mexico essays.

What Maclean has attempted, in *Young Men and Fire,* is nothing less than a redefinition of tragedy for the spaces of the West, where "screwups and blowups" are paramount, and the "first and last question of life" is "How did it happen?," as well as for the era of wind tunnels and mushroom clouds. So it was a delight to me to find part of his thought echoed in the most cosmopolitan of modern commentators on tragedy, a commentator, moreover, who firmly believes tragedy is dead in the modern world. George Steiner writes: "[A]ny realistic notion of the tragic must start from the fact of catastrophe. Tragedies end badly. The tragic personage is broken by forces which can neither be fully understood nor overcome by rational prudence. . . . [E]ven where the moralist could point to a particular crime or occasion of disaster, a more general law [i]s at work." Not only in the Wild West, but everywhere, "[o]utside and within man is *l'autre,* the "otherness" of the world. Call it what you will: a hidden or malevolent God, blind fate, the solicitations of hell, or the brute fury of our animal blood. It waits for us at the crossroads. It mocks and destroys us. In certain rare instances, it leads us after destruction to some incomprehensible repose."[10]

*   *   *   *

Part of what I have come to understand, in making this double journey with Norman Maclean, through his criticism and his art, is why he went back to Montana, and why he was an Aristotelian. A concern with the nuts and bolts of art must have come easily to a woodsman, who knew that "little details" can have big consequences. But his concentration on them implied no reductiveness, rather an extreme humility before the difficulties of an art he was, all his life, hesitating to undertake. In the "Lear" essay, he applies his inimitable dry humor to the condescension of academics, while at the same time registering his own trepidation: "For, to speak of an artistic attainment as possessing magnitude in the highest degree is to imply the existence of attainments somewhat analogous and in this and that common respect somewhat inferior; it either implies this or the existence of a critic who has some a priori concept of a poem more wonderful than any yet written, in which case the critic should change to a more wonderful profession and contribute its culminating splendor." Maclean did turn to that "more wonderful profession," but with a combination of humility and astuteness for which his whole career as a teacher and sometime critic had been a preparation. The difficulty of art, as he always knew, cannot escape technique, yet must transcend technique. For the aim of art is nothing less than to "transfer 'life' from flesh to words" ("Lear," 95–96).

China Trade (II)

Moving into the Bay Area poetry scene in the early 1980s was a heady experience. If I brought with me any eastern prejudices and misgivings about a laid-back, anti-intellectual West, they were quickly exploded. The poetic elders, whose rare readings were a centering event for the whole community, were Czeslaw Milosz and Robert Duncan—great omnivorous souls, in whom history and learning were inextricably interwoven with vision and personal sorrow. George Oppen was still alive, and the quickness and severity of his objectivism were being handed down through poets like Carl Rakosi and Jack Marshall. The young poets at UC Berkeley were more likely to be influenced by the Yvor Winters tradition—as enlarged by Thom Gunn and Robert Pinsky—than by, say, Ferlinghetti. The polemics I had been engaged in, against the emotional and intellectual slackness of the "surrealism" still popular in the mid-American MFA programs, out here seemed— as a Berkeley poet quickly told me—not wrong, but simply beside the point. I had come out, instead, in a kind of reverse universe from that of Cambridge, Massachusetts, one where the objects of curiosity were quite different, but the ideals of intellectual and visionary reach the same. Poets my age seemed to share a kind of lingua franca—allusions to Buddhism, or to gnosticism and the Christian heresies, a concern for spiritual search, and a slightly orientalizing mode of description—making them more comprehensible to each other, and perhaps a little less to the outside world.

In this chapter, I shall touch on only a few of the poets I encountered at that time—not even, necessarily, the best, but those who particularly exemplify this shared atmosphere.

Peter Dale Scott is a retired professor of English at UC Berkeley, a former diplomat, a fairly celebrated investigator of assassinations and conspiracies, and (still) a Canadian, not a U.S., citizen. He was involved in translation projects with Milosz until the Vietnam War and Milosz's vehement anticommunism separated them. He has become, over the years, an increasingly serious meditator, in the Zen and Vipassana traditions. It was for its new way of writing about meditation—as well as for the omnivorous curiosity it shares with its precursor, *Coming to Jakarta*—that his second autobiographical long poem, *Listening to the Candle*, first seized my interest:

> Each morning
> for a few stolen minutes
> on *zafu* and *zabuton*
>
> beyond Maylie to the right
> I listen to the wet
> commuter traffic
>
> the window occasionally trembling
> in front of my half-closed eyes
> as a truck changes gears
>
> and six inches to my left
> the wall-silence
> a flatness not heard
>
> till the sparrow's notes
> fall deeper inside my brain
> than I would once have dared
>
> he was there then
> in the spindly sumac
> the granite too hard and old
>
> for fossils or inscription
> my father is dying
> what would I have without these birds?[1]

Listening to the Candle is not a pious Buddhist tract, by any means; its next-to-last section details the scandals of various sanghas in the Far West and places the poet squarely among those "whose limit . . . is a sense of well-being / not of non-being." But the very absence of dogma allows the poem to get, in its wonderful Williams-like slippages, the odd vagary of meditation—wandering over trivial learning and a lifetime's forgotten experience—as many more committed poets have not. It is more psychological and emotional than previous meditative poetry, open to the moments of private desolation that can sweep over the meditator but also to the fundamental insight: that it takes "dar[ing]"—but brings immense restoration—to let down the screens of mental processing, of unvoiced storytelling, that all our culture teaches us to be most comfortable within, and simply be where we are.

Listening to the Candle is written at a time when academic fashion believes that the storytelling is all: that "beyond language" there is at best a crying absence, a Lacanian lack. Scott can be scathing about the ego-driven territoriality of these departmental certainties:

> the debates of mystery
> and collegial discourse

> dating back to the Middle Ages
> whether *god has three selves*
> or *the author none*

This *"neurotic Cartesian / quest for certainty,"* Scott says, has been "used yet again to exclude" the truly venturesome, "those who might correct / our reluctance to expand / towards the boundaries of mind." Yet Scott is too much the conspiracy-prober, the distruster of appearances, quite to dismiss the argument from social construction, or to posit a unitary self. Scott has, indeed, a charming way of moving through both sides of almost any argument. Even the possibility that the various forms of illiteracy, economic crisis, and disinformation have put us on the edge of a new Dark Age—commonly a conservative, not a radical theme—is entertained, but leads Scott to remember how much the Dark Ages generated out of their concentration on their "one Book." Scott's method is nowhere more meditative than in these assertions of nondualism, this faith that wholeness of mind is a process of moving through opposite perspectives, not a clinging to one side. He reminds us of the social—the subtle impact of power—whenever we are inclined to overvalue art, privacy, freedom.

When current debates become too real, he reminds us of immediacy: "the muttering candle / at the point of going out / the cat distending on the rug."

In literary debates, Scott is, again, nondualistic. He remains loyal to Robert Duncan's aesthetic of open form, for resisting the "civilization" that can be equated with "denial" by *keep[ing] our exposure / to what we do not know.*" But he draws back from the other emerging West Coast avant-garde that would *"deny / the possibility / of a project/ larger than its language,"* pointing out how convenient an aesthetic of *"nose-thumbing"* can be for the political mystifiers who deal seriously, if ferociously, with questions of value. It is perhaps the balance between open form, tireless intellectual voyaging, and a certain dogged humanism, that gives Scott's work its peculiar power to captivate.

*   *   *   *

Jane Hirshfield is perhaps the most widely read avowedly Buddhist poet in Northern California, after Snyder. She takes the risky though rewarding tactic of offering explicit advice or wisdom— rewarding in that it attracts a wider audience, risky in that it breaks the poetry world's own taboos and awakens that world's hypersensitivity to cliche and complacency. To my taste, the key of Hirschfield's success, especially in her most recent book, *Given Sugar, Given Salt,* is her awareness that "Neither a person entirely broken / nor one entirely whole can speak."[2] If the reminder that no speaker is "entirely broken" covertly challenges the negative stereotypes with which "confessional" poetry has been burdened, the reminder that no speaker is "entirely whole," while challenging complete religious detachment as an artistic ideal, also cautions against the kind of advice-giving that proclaims its own health along with its moral, leaving behind the divided, conflicted person in whom the need for a moral began.

So Hirshfield's poetry seems least satisfying to me, though sometimes charming, when it belabors the Buddhist truism that "Everyday mind is the way," speaking, for instance, of "the sigh of happiness / each object gives off / if I glimpse for even an instant the actual instant" ("Only When I Am Quiet and Do Not Speak"). (Though perhaps it's the Rilkean echoes that bother me in these lines, as much as the reassuring message.) Better are the poems that simply, but inventively, record a moment, and let the gasp of recognition come by itself:

> They remind of the walnut's almost welded-in sweetness.
> They remind of the unbribable cat.
> They remind of the roof, its sloped unconcern for above
> or below.   ("Elephant Seals, Ano Nuevo Preserve")

Best of all are the poems that remind us that "Balance is noticed most when almost failed of" ("Balance"); that deal in human recognitions that are both very liberating and very painful. One such poem is "The Silence," which begins with the recognition that many friends of a recently dead person may have felt, like the speaker, that they truly knew him only by one shared confidence. Should the speaker take this darkly, as a sign of how little we know of each other, how little we seize our only moment; or, more positively, as showing how the "flavor / of how much I know of others" goes on forever,

> Each secret separate, different,
> leading its life now without him:
> carrying laundry, washing the windows, straightening up.

Contemplating these divided truths, "Love . . . quietly listens" but also, nondualistically, "lowers its stricken face so no one will see."

*   *   *   *

No one would accuse Brenda Hillman's work of claiming entire wholeness. Its outside religious perspective comes not from the Far East but from gnosticism, with its so seemingly un-Californian view that "suffering" is "inherent in matter," and our souls are an immaterial "light" waiting for liberation into another realm.[3] Yet this view, paradoxically, allows a rare acceptance of the "Californian," in the sense of the new, the tacky, the superficial, if only because older or more rigorous forms of the aesthetic wouldn't embody the Absolute, either. After a visit to Disneyland, a typical Hillman speaker concludes affectionately, almost ecstatically, that "reality wore that same / sweet shabbiness."[4] She cherishes the flimsy, the constructed, as if they were metaphysical gates onto the Void, or fullness, beyond. (It is no wonder that Wayne Thiebaud is one of her favorite painters.) And, like Tomas Transtromer, she makes connections across boundary lines more conventional poets keep rigid—nature and culture, the anthropomorphic and the objective. Who else would see *whales* smiling with "the weak little smile of exhausted history"? Or hear a foghorn's "major third downward" as a voice calling a child: "John-ny! Mar-y!"?[5]

Hillman's perspective allows the stereotyped mores she observes to be an object not of satire but of compassion. We see what is hopelessly generic, but also what is frightened and hopeful, when

>all the divorced Californians
>start out to the Point with their bottled waters
>in their fragile foreign cars ("A Foghorn")

Their whale-watching becomes the "call" that is "heard in all the great systems," where "The sleepy ones have gathered at the shore / to proclaim the glamour of the alien sun." If whatever is "alien" seems to call out "Come home," it is not just because of our restless or decadent need for "glamour," our corrupt affection for the nature we hold in our strangling grasp, but because in the gnostic view all incarnation is unsatisfactory, in need of the "disembodied voice" that reminds it of the unsayable wholeness that is elsewhere, or nowhere, or everywhere. This view dignifies what might seem melodramatic or self-indulgent in the middle-class Californians' view of themselves and their predicament: "divorced from [their] lives, and from this century. . . . shouldn't something have pity on them now?"

I suspect the poignancy of poems like "A Foghorn" may pall on some readers, making them wish for the Zen poets' less emotional, stick-thumping emphasis on thusness. Perhaps Hillman's decision, in her recent work, to be influenced by the randomness and irony of L=A=N=G=U=A=G=E poetry is a kind of self-corrective to the dominance of such emotions. But there is a rare, unique humor to her visions as well, as in "The Rat," where, after she has treated her pet rat as an escape from work, a "son," a lover almost, "let[ting him . . . lie for hours on my inadequate breast,"

>then he starts this purring or clicking
>such as must occur

at the center of the universe,
the sound acacias make when they split
their seeds on a hot day

It is indeed a new world, one visible from no other perspective.

*   *   *   *

Of course, the poet in my generation who has most put his stamp on Northern California landscapes is Robert Hass. His relation to the Far East is ambiguous; he has never explicitly associated himself with any form of Buddhism. But his long views of the Golden Gate and the Marin County uplands have the proportions and the serenity of Japanese prints. In his marvelous essay on haiku, "Images," he imagines himself casting Berkeley life into that genre—"Beach towels drying in the moonlight"—and being told by one of his heroes, "Hass, you have Edo taste" ("Edo" implying overdecorative, self-conscious).[6]

What the California landscape embodies, for Hass, is not majesty, as in Jeffers, or a transhuman alertness, as in Snyder, but a mellow clarity, a late-afternoon warmth in which longing is bounded, life is found acceptable:

Sweet smell of timothy in the meadow.
Clouds massing east above the ridge in a sky
as blue as the mountain lakes,
so there are places on this earth clear all the way up
and all the way down
and in between a various blossoming[7]

This mellowness of temperament, combined with a suave, but distinctly populist, left-wing intellectuality—an epitome of the best of Berkeley in the 1960s—has won Hass an immense audience, and a few doubters and detractors. His recent poem "My Mother's Nipples"—his best, in my opinion, since the famous "Meditation at Lagunitas"—suggests that he himself has become one of the doubters; that is to say, inclined to measure the peace he can imagine so persuasively against the waste and pain in his own life, and in his culture's. His poem begins with the meadows he has described being bulldozed, then replaced with a housing development called "Squaw Valley Meadows." This grim instance of signifiers replacing signifieds will reverberate throughout. The central story in the poem, the poet's mother's, is one of profound cultural poverty: a forced marriage (kept secret for a lifetime); suburban proprieties and evasions; then alcoholism, then hospitalizations. . . . This version of California life almost makes me think of Frank Bidart, Hass's opposite in so many ways, when he writes

> The brown house
> on the brown hill
> reminds me of my parents.

> Its memory is of poverty,
> not merely poverty of means,
> but poverty of history, of awareness of
> the ways men have found to live.[8]

In Hass's poem, the mother's story is so bald and unforgiving that, after one or two brief essays in lines, it demands to be told as prose—a crisp, novelistic prose with all of Hass's eye for odd detail but none of his suspect smoothness. Again and again, these passages break up the passages framed as poetry, in which nature and learning seem to promise a refuge, almost to persuade the poet that he has encompassed psychic wholeness. His efforts to regroup, to do justice both to pain and to happiness, take the form of a series of refrain lines, endlessly rewritten:

> I said to myself:
> some things do not blossom in this life.

> I said: what we've lost is a story
> and what we've never had
> a song.

But this doesn't seem adequate, either to "what we've lost" or to what we have. The next version is more optimistic, but more confused:

> What we've never had is a song
> and what we've really had is a song.

The last rewritings, and the prose passage that interrupts them, are so heartbreaking they demand to be quoted in full:

I said: there are all kinds of emptiness and fullness
that sing and do not sing.

I said: you are her singing.

I came home from school and she was gone. I don't know
what instinct sent me to the park. I suppose it was the
only place I could think of where someone might hide: she
had passed out under an orange tree, curled up. Her face,
flushed, eyelids swollen, was a ruin. Though I needed
urgently to know whatever was in it, I could hardly bear
to look. When I couldn't wake her, I decided to sit with
her until she woke up. I must have been ten years old: I
suppose I wanted for us to look like a son and mother who
had been picnicking, like a mother who had fallen asleep
in the warm light and scent of orange blossoms and a boy
who was sitting beside her daydreaming, not thinking
about anything in particular.

You are not her singing, though she is what's
broken in a song.
She is its silences.

She may be its silences.

The poet cannot, finally, contain the mother's pain, or his own
childish need to make it something different, in anything he has
made. (Even "She is its silences" has to be restated and qualified
with a "may be.") Can he then separate his own brilliantly rendered mellow fullness, which does return in the succeeding
lines—"Hawk drifting in the blue air"—from the boy's defensive
"daydreaming"? At the end,

I tried to think of some place on earth she loved

I remember she only ever spoke happily
of high school.

The mother must be left—at best!—in her own sweetly, shal-
lowly social world; the poet cannot meet her on his own grounds,
of happiness or of self-examination. And so the poem ends in an
absolute stand-off, which is, of course, far more powerful, more a
form of being-where-one-is, than any resolution could be. It goes

far beyond the issues of the local culture, into the old problem all religions, all therapies, must face—all efforts to resolve the pain of life on the ground of vision.

The poem is not free of the kind of intellectual-earthy pyrotechnics that will please Hass's fans, and probably put off his detractors. Much of the first third is taken up with the parodic songs various kinds of poets would write about "les nipples de ma mere." But even here, there is "*The indigenist's song*," for which much can be forgiven. It is a purported vision-quest, in which "the boy they called Loves His Mother's Tits" goes into the mountains and fasts for six days.

> On the seventh he made three deep cuts
> In the meat of his palm. He entered the pain at noon
> And an eagle came to him crying three times like the
> mewling
> A doe makes planting her hooves in the soft duff for
> mating
> And he went home and they called him Eagle Three
> Times after that.

It's a lovely send-up of West Coast poetry's own cliches, its sometimes presumptuous cooptations of the primitive; and at the same time it is a little epitome of the poem's whole drama, and its basic question. What is the point of "displacement," universal though it may be? What is the point of despising and renaming psychic need, even if the new name is maleness or transcendence? These questions return, in a way, to Hass's early left-wing distrust of cultural superstructures; but they also cast doubt on his own claim to unity with nature, leaving him irrevocably in the camp of the pained, driven culture-makers.

This is important to note because some eastern critics have overemphasized the "Californian" mellowness in Hass and others of his generation. Their frame of reference, it is true, is different from that of other poetic constituencies. But the irony, the pain, the far-reaching rumination—even the hints of deconstruction—in their best poems defeat simplistic categorization. As I discovered when I moved to Berkeley in 1983, this work is not less, but differently, intellectual than East Coast poetry; not less, but differently, perplexed about the heart.

Always Coming Home

I am thinking about two equal and opposite human desires. They are, it seems to me, universal and inescapable, though recent western literature has often tried mightily to choose one to the exclusion of the other. The first might be called the cosmopolitan impulse. It is the desire to see what is beyond one's immediate horizon, whatever that may be; ultimately, to know the world, to have been everywhere, to have all the possibilities, all the freedoms, of the various human cultures available to one. It could also be called the desire to be, in the fullest sense of the word, an individual. In the Italian Renaissance, when the ideal of individualism was most strongly formulated, a humanist was expected not to be particularly bound to any one locality. (Since many humanists were political exiles, this was partly making a virtue of necessity.) Jacob Burckhardt, in *The Civilization of the Renaissance in Italy*, has many quotations like "My country is the whole world"—that is Dante—or "Only he who has learned everything is nowhere a stranger."[1] I think none of us, if we are honest, will find this impulse to be unbounded alien, when we are thinking about the narrownesses of particular cultures. Women in Islamic societies, I have been told, find it comforting just to know of the existence of western feminism. And we in the West, where the metaphysical choices have often seemed to be between the facts of science and the pseudofacts of one or another fundamentalism, have found it liberating to learn that in the Far East "religion" can mean a state of consciousness or intuition about Being, with no "facts" at all—no anthropomorphic Creator, no Judge, no Hell, and even, in some cases, no Heaven.

And yet, most of us will recognize another dream: the dream of living in one place, knowing every detail of its topography, its flora and fauna, marrying someone one has known all one's life, seeing one's grandchildren play under the same trees that figure in one's own earliest memories, until there seems no boundary between one's self and the world that has made it. Movies and popular novels have made this image luminous to us; and however much they also tell us about the bigotry and boredom in small towns, the young people's eagerness to leave, the image remains, and for us cosmopolitans, often symbolizes unity of being— a mind that is embodied, in a world that is real.

So we are, many of us, in the same position as Thea Kronborg in Willa Cather's *The Song of the Lark*, "pulled in two, between the desire to go away forever and the desire to stay forever."[2] Certainly my own life history has made it utterly impossible for me to choose between the two ideals. I have belonged—and still do belong—to too many landscapes. The imprinted landscape of my childhood was Chicago, if anywhere; yet Chicago for me inextricably also represented the cosmopolitan ideal. Call it, in a phrase whose resonances will appear presently, the City of Mind. Perhaps it was because so many of its wonders looked outward or inward, onto the farthest depths of reality. The old, disused stadium—now torn down—under whose stands the first nuclear chain reaction took place. The dinosaur room in the Field Museum, scary because its darkest point, midway between the two doors at the far ends, was just where one had to walk past the fully mounted, free-standing bones of brontosaurus. The Planetarium, out on a spit in Lake Michigan, whose scale-models, I saw on a recent visit, now show not the nearest stars, but the nearest galaxies.

But more probably, I felt about Chicago as I did because it was where my father had his identity as a shy, distinguished man of letters. His more troubled loyalty to his rural and western roots had too much in common with the standards by which the "toughs" judged me at school. So that his own dislike for the city, his happiness at leaving it every summer, were always a bit of a threat. In Chicago, I knew that I would eventually escape those standards, find more and more sophisticated elites where the way I was was not only acceptable, but the norm.

And yet, even in the city, the other ideal crept in, not only as a threat, but as an elusive promise. It was there that my teacher actually did say—as I have recorded in a poem—that if I grew up sexually I might "give it all up, get married, go and work in the steel mills"—and that such a fate might be a kind of mystic union with my "chemistry." It was there in the cottonwood trees that still lined the streets of Hyde Park, taller than the apartment buildings they stood next to, and in the fantasy that the rays of light that slunk through them, before anyone was up on early summer mornings, were Indian braves slipping through a recovered forest, still the guardians of the place's healing essence, as they are in Hart Crane's great poem "The Dance."

What mediated between the two principles, in my childhood, was travel. Our cross-country trips every summer held our family's divided identities in a briefly happy suspension. They swallowed us up in the land, in remoter and remoter places that some people probably never did leave in a lifetime. But in itself travel was like the mind, tasting the places, sifting, comparing them, always leaving them behind. In our attachment to it, we were not atypical. Travel *is* a place for Americans, children of the frontier, believers in perpetual possibility. The poet Robert Pinsky has put this very eloquently—at the same time casting doubt on the very duality of "motion" and "place"—in his long poem *An Explanation of America*:

> And motion would be a place, and who knows, you
> May live there in the famous national "love
> Of speed" as though in some small town where children
> Walk past their surnames in the churchyard. . . .
> For *place*, itself, is always a kind of motion,
> A part of it artificial and preserved,
> And a part born in a blur of loss and change—[3]

Western ecological writings have, in recent decades, made a choice between the two principles that Pinsky, and I, find so ineluctable. They have opted, overwhelmingly, in favor of the principle of locality, of "bioregionalism" or "reinhabitation." No doubt this is largely in response to the danger that American, or globalized, mass culture—the ubiquitous MacDonalds, the video store, the satellite TV dish—will homogenize local difference almost out of existence. It is also, in a way, an act of reparation, through emulation, toward the locally centered Native American cultures we have displaced and destroyed. Robert Hass as Poet Laureate—inspired by Gary Snyder—initiated a program in which schoolchildren all over the country have had to learn what watershed they live in, and the implications of thinking about their environment in those terms. David Robertson's recent criticism also groups artists by watershed or "ecosystem," subordinating the claims of the one or two the cosmopolitan world considers "great" to the community of local practice they arose from. We seem close to the Tao Te Ching's vision of the ideal society, as translated, with evident relish, by another West Coast writer, Stephen Mitchell:

> There may be a few wagons or boats,
> but these don't go anywhere.
> There may be an arsenal of weapons,
> but nobody ever uses them
>
> . . . .
>
> And even though the next country is so close
> that people can hear its roosters crowing and its dogs
>   barking,
> they are content to die of old age
> without ever having gone to see it.[4]

And yet, I would argue that much of the classic literature of the American West still finds the problem of the local and the universal difficult, as difficult as I found it in childhood. Let me take two examples, one from the beginning, one from the end of the twentieth century.

Willa Cather's *The Song of the Lark* is the story of Thea Kronborg from Moonstone, Colorado, who becomes a world-famous opera singer. The love of the local clearly has a strong voice in this book. Physically, Moonstone is a wonder-world, like the Archbishop's Acoma or Lawrence's Taos. Its eponyms, the moon and rare stones, dominate more scenes than one cares to count. The sand hills outside of town, with their "crystals and agates and onyx, and petrified wood as red as blood," and the mica-laden plains have a "glare . . . more intense than the rays from above." The sky "look[s] like blue lava, forever incapable of clouds" (39, 59). Transformation reigns in the desert mirage and seems to open onto endless reaches of time. The reflections of heifers "were magnified to a preposterous height and looked like mammoths, prehistoric beasts standing solitary in the water that for many thousands of years actually washed over the desert" (38).

But morally, Moonstone presents a very different landscape. "The fear of the tongue, that terror of little towns," governs everything (101). Any unusual behavior, or behavior that represents a claim to individual singularity, is severely censured. Moonstone's religion, as epitomized in Thea's sister, Anna, is largely a matter of self-important disapproval of others, disguised prurience, a "fishy curiosity which justifies itself by an expression of horror." Religious considerations are rarely distinguished from an ironclad respect for social caste. Anna disapproves of Thea's suitor Ray because he is an "atheist," but even more because "he was not a passenger conductor with brass buttons on his coat" (106). And "Mexicans and sinners" are treated as virtual synonyms (48).

Probably most readers will remember most vividly one particular instance of Moonstone's exclusionary ethic, and its consequences. An ugly, foul-smelling tramp comes to town and is rejected by everyone, even Thea, who "put[s] her handkerchief to her nose" (108). In the end, the tramp teaches the town a terrible lesson in human brotherhood: he drowns himself in the town water-tank, causing a typhoid epidemic. Thea is thrown into a religious crisis, less about God's justice than about her fellow townspeople's. She says to her beloved friend Doctor Archie: "It seems to me . . . that the whole town's to blame. I'm to blame, myself. . . . There's not one person in Moonstone that really lives the way the New Testament says" (110–11). The story, however, reflects not only on the hypocrisy of Christian ethics but on the dark side of the local, of community itself—its need to found its self-definition, its sense of security, on the exclusion of something other.

Even Doctor Archie can offer Thea only an oblique consolation. He too believes that no one could live up to the New Testament precepts literally. Instead, he offers a doctrine of individualistic escape and self-cultivation: "the failures are swept back into the pile and forgotten. . . . The people who forge ahead and do something, they really count" (111).

Dr. Archie belongs to a kind of Nietzschean elite of the self-defined in Moonstone, men who recognize each other, even if they do not always entirely approve of each other. There is Professor Wunsch, the alcoholic, almost derelict piano teacher, who finds in Thea an artistic "seriousness" he had despaired of ever encountering again (24). There is Spanish Johnny, whose passion for the mandolin carries him off periodically to sing in bars throughout the Southwest and Mexico, coming back to his wife at last exhausted and half-alive. There is Ray Kennedy, the railroadman, who, though the most conventional, earns the category by his atheism and his "adventurous life in New Mexico and the Southwest" (37).

All of these men—as Wunsch's name ("wish," in German) might indicate—have a quality of unfulfilled, perhaps unfulfillable longing about them. It—and the synecdochic quality of longing itself—are most memorably summed up when Spanish Johnny's wife, trying to explain his wanderings, holds up a shell to Doctor Archie's ear: "You hear the sea; and yet the sea is very far from here. You have judgment, and you know that. But he is fooled. To him, it is the sea itself." And Thea, holding the shell to her ear, can herself hear "something calling one," and therefore "something awe-inspiring" (36).

It is no small part of the pathos of the book that this longing, in at least three of these men, is focused on Thea before she is twelve years old. Quite simply, there is no one else. For a writer whom lesbian feminism is eager to annex, Cather's portrait of the young Anglo women of Moonstone is ferocious indeed. Only the dying consumptives at the Wednesday evening prayer meeting have a shred of nobility or introspection. The others are either monsters of self-important piety, like Anna, or master strategists of the popularity-and-marriage game, like Mrs. Archie and her younger equivalent, Lily Fisher.

If Cather's experience as a sexual outsider shows anywhere in this book, I would say, it is in the delicate sympathy with which the irregular side of the three men's affection for Thea is handled. I've had students note, and be shocked by, a "pedophilic" theme in the book—Doctor Archie's feeling about "what a beautiful thing a young girl's body was . . . so neatly and delicately fashioned," especially as it is closely juxtaposed to the information that "His marriage was a very unhappy one" (8). But surely the tone in which Cather both recognizes the erotic feeling and sees how it is subsumed in the larger reality of Doctor Archie's generosity, bespeaks precisely that "delicacy that goes with a nature of warm impulses" that Cather opposes to Anna's "fishy curiosity" (106).

But in the larger design of the book, the pathos of the men's situation is only a small part of the point. What is important is that they provide Thea with her escape-velocity: Ray by his death and his bequest; Dr. Archie by his encouragement, and later in more practical ways; Wunsch and Spanish Johnny by their artistic standards, and their recognition of Thea's talent.

Thea does escape. Yet the irony of the book is that the great world, though necessary, proves in some ways even more meager in its possibilities—the good voice teacher who is a narrow and cynical human being, the wealthy suitor who neglects to mention that he is already married. Perhaps the exclusion and death of the tramp would not happen so easily in Chicago; but still, "Jessie Darcey"—the popular though frequently off-key singer— "was only Lily Fisher under another name" (208).

And here the principle of locality dialectically reasserts itself. Though Thea can no longer return to Moonstone, it is through a pilgrimage back to the West, to the Anasazi ruins of Panther Canyon, that she comes to terms with the limitation of all human lives and acquires the courage to endure what greatness requires. Even her lover must finally acknowledge: "Her scale of values will always be the Moonstone scale. And, with an artist, that *is* an advantage."

And yet, though Thea triumphs, the book cannot finally be called triumphant. Rather, it is a kind of Jamesian hourglass. When Thea is young, the "people who go through in the dining car," who seem so different, are the fantasy-locus of all that is rich and promising in the world (33). As Thea's life narrows almost entirely to the practice and discipline of her art—and her irritability rises, to the point that she spends hours silently raging at her "nigger" laundress—Moonstone itself becomes that locus; she puts herself to sleep imagining her childhood room and her father's house, "everyone . . . warm and well downstairs" (358–59). In this sense, longing remains forever synecdochic; what one does not have is always needed to complete what one has.

Finally, one must acknowledge, though cautiously and with reluctance, that in one sense Thea fails. She pours all her talents into a received art form, one that has everything to do with Europe and its already outlived, stylized myths, and nothing to do with the American West. One makes this point cautiously, because Cather is no anti-intellectual of the kind so common among the minor boosters of western literature. She knows that to find, and to understand, a high art form—*any* high art form—is from one point of view the only thing that matters. Yet I raise the point anyway because Thea herself seems to dream of a further step. Hearing, for the first time, Dvorak's *New World* Symphony, she feels "[t]his was . . . music from the New World indeed! Strange how, as the first movement wore on, it brought back to her that high tableland above Laramie; the grass-grown wagon-trails, the faraway peaks of the snowy range, the wind and the eagles, that old man and the first telegraph message" (158–59). Thea herself will create no work that thus explicitly synthesizes high art and American experience; though, one need hardly say, Cather intends to create one, in imagining her.

*   *   *   *

And yet, I think *The Song of the Lark* does achieve a moment of resolution between the antinomies of the local and the universal, in Thea's visit to Panther Canyon. Thea comes to the Anasazi ruins at the point when she is most "tired" of her own "personality," as it has been shaped by her aspirations in, and bargains with, the Great World. Yet the landscape seems to speak to her both of the necessity, and of the limits, of individuation. "The great pines stand at a considerable distance from each other. Each tree grows alone, murmurs alone, thinks alone." Yet in their presence Thea feels relieved of "personality," of the "old, fretted lines which marked one off, which defined her" (233).

One might as well call what Thea learns at Panther Canyon a form of meditative practice. Sitting alone all day, in the nest she has made herself in the cliff-dwelling, she "wonder[s] at her own inactivity," feeling that "All her life she had been hurrying and sputtering, as if she had been born behind time and had been trying to catch up. Now . . . it was as if she were waiting for something to catch up with her. . . . Here she could lie for half a day undistracted, holding pleasant and incomplete conceptions in her mind—almost in her hands. They were scarcely clear enough to be called ideas. They had something to do with fragrance and colour and sound, but almost nothing to do with words. . . . [H]er power to think seemed converted into a power of sustained sensation" (236–37).

It is the mode of thinking Buddhism calls Big Mind, a mode that, as it loses the distinction between thinking and perceiving, also loses the distinction between subject and object: "She could become a mere receptacle for heat, or become a colour." Very gradually, this mode of being proves to have some relevance to the artistic aspirations Thea has so resolutely turned her back on. "[A] song would go through her head all morning, as a spring keeps welling up," but without any need for ideas of striving and mastery.

Yet the Anasazi also bring her back to an awareness of basic human destiny, at its most universal, physical level, and therefore of the necessity, in another sense, of struggle. She remembers Ray Kennedy's musings about how "the hardness of the [ancient people's] struggle . . . made one feel an obligation to do one's best" (238). Finally one morning she has a revelation, one that brings together history and prehistory, process and product, art and life. "The stream and the broken pottery: what was any art but an effort to make a sheath, a mold in which to imprison for a moment the shining, elusive element which is life itself—life hurrying past us and running away, too strong to stop, too sweet to lose?" Art and nature, or embodied existence, are no longer opposites, but the same thing. To sing is nothing more than to be fully, consciously, alive and transitory. "In singing, one made a vessel of one's throat and nostrils and held it on one's breath, caught the stream in a scale of natural intervals" (240).

As meditators know, Big Mind has an uncanny way of resolving practical problems before one's consciousness is even aware they are at issue. It is astonishing how quickly Thea's worldly plans reshape themselves, once she has had her insight. She will not "teach music in little country towns all her life," as she has resigned herself to doing (234); "she was going to Germany to study without further loss of time" (242). Germany might seem the very opposite of the emotional locus of Panther Canyon; in the dialectical structure of the novel, it is not. Once Thea knows what her art *is*, she knows unerringly what it requires of her.

Gesang ist Dasein, Rilke would soon be writing, in the German language, thousands of miles east of Panther Canyon—"Singing is being." This doesn't mean any easy cult of spontaneity, "first thought best thought," for him any more than for Thea. For he goes on to ask, "But when can we truly *be*?"[5]

The difficult task of truly being, and its relation to art, is what Thea learns at Panther Canyon. It may also be what the literature of the West is most preoccupied with learning, in its delicate balances between Europe and the Far East, and (though they are not the same!) the intellectual and the anti-intellectual. But it can't be put firmly on either side of the dialectic of the local and the universal. For Thea, it is inextricably entwined with the reaffirmation of a native place, of "things which seemed destined for her" (237). Yet it also includes—and must include—her imagination's freedom to journey back six hundred years; the spirit's freedom to love vastness, to "flow through the galaxies," to quote Gary Snyder's translation of Han Shan.[6] That is why it is something Thea can carry with her wherever she goes. The duality proves to be—like all dualities, from the Buddhist point of view—in the last issue illusory.

*   *   *   *

It intrigues me, then, to discover a similar dialectic in a book that might seem the ultimate bioregionalist text, Ursula Le Guin's *Always Coming Home.* Le Guin, as most readers will know, was the daughter of the Kroebers, famous for the Berkeley Anthropological Museum and for *Ishi: Last of His Tribe.* Her parents' Native American "informants" were part of the family's summer household in the Napa Valley. She tells affectionate but, from current perspectives, slightly troubling stories about them: how one, to prove to the children that "Injuns don't get poison oak," plunged chest-deep into a patch of it.

It's tempting to view Le Guin's later career as a science fiction writer as a continuation of her parents' anthropology by different means. Always there are two invented cultures to compare, split along recurring but shifting axes of primitive/civilized, socialist/ capitalist, intuitive/rationalist, matriarchal/ patriarchal. Most are set on imaginary planets throughout the cosmos; but when Le Guin came to *Always Coming Home*, which she thought of explicitly as a "utopia," she set it on earth. At first, it was placed in the high Andes, among the Quechua (whence the name "Kesh"). But at a certain point, Le Guin says, she realized "it had to be my valley" and located it in Napa, changing the topography only slightly, so that fans wouldn't go and gawk at the "real" Sinshan or Ounmalin.[7] Thus the title refers to Le Guin's own imaginative homecoming, as well as to an ideal for the human journey.

So. In the Napa Valley, thousands of years after some nuclear or ecological catastrophe has "poisoned" much of the earth, live the Kesh. They are not a numerous people, partly because of deliberate family planning, partly because they have inherited a fatal neurological disease from the catastrophe. Though they have a short railroad, and even a "finders [explorers] lodge," most of them are like the people in the Tao Te Ching, "content to die of old age" without ever having seen the neighboring country.

The Kesh represent an ideal of centeredness, in one's place and in the world, as their term for their ancestors of the age of civilization—"when they lived outside the world"—might indicate.[8] Their metaphor for these ancestors—"a human being with its head on backwards" (159)—unconsciously echoes, and opposes, a trope in Rilke's *Duino Elegies* for a necessary difference between animal and human consciousness:

> With all its eyes the natural world looks out
> into the Open. Only *our* eyes are turned
> backward, and surround plant, animal, child
> like traps, as they emerge into their freedom.

Human beings, Rilke says, see only *Gestaltung* (a complex word that implies a preexisting construction or interpretation) and therefore cannot see "what is really out there." LeGuin's Kesh will attempt to present an alternative model of humanity.[9]

The Kesh seem a composite of the Native American cultures the Kroebers studied, along with certain purely utopian elements. Most things are owned in common; giving, not hoarding, is the Kesh definition of wealth. Households and families are organized matrilineally. Their religion is animist: like Lawrence's Hopi, the Kesh have no divinities but believe the whole world is alive and

155

in communication with them. They have a rich artistic life, but no canon; few works are preserved in written form beyond the generation that produced them. Their governing symbol, applied to all areas of life, is the "heyiya-if," two balancing curves, rather like Yin and Yang, but not touching each other at any point. It speaks to a basic faith in indeterminacy, as well as in a dance of opposites that can, and must, reverse.

In opposition to the Kesh—since Le Guin's novels, like the heyiya-if, are built around contraries—are the Condor people. Formerly nomadic, now empire-building, like Europe's own presumed "Aryan" ancestors from the steppes, they do not respond to the landscape but impose their own rectilinear order on it. They constitute a kind of Swiftian satire on monotheism and patriarchy, combining the worst characteristics of Christianity, Islam, the Roman Empire, and America in the Reagan years. Or, to invoke a different eighteenth-century writer, they are a textbook proof of William Blake's contention that transcendental monotheism and an authoritarian social order go together: "One King, one God, one Law." The heroine Stone Telling, who is half-Kesh, half-Condor, sums up their belief-system thus:

> One made everything out of nothing. One is a person, immortal. He is all-powerful. Human men are imitations of him. One is not the universe; he made it, and gives it orders. Things are not part of him nor is he part of them, so you must not praise things, but only One. The One, however, reflects himself in the Condor [the emperor]; so the Condor is to be praised and obeyed. And the True Condors and One-Warriors, who are all called Sons of the Condor or Sons of the Son, are reflections of the reflection of One, and therefore also to be praised and obeyed. The tyon [peasants] are very dim and faint reflections far removed from One, but even so they have enough of his power to be called human beings. No other people [in the Kesh language, "people" includes animals] are human. The hontik, that is women and foreigners and animals, have nothing to do with One at all; they are purutik, unclean, dirt people. They were made by One to obey and serve the Sons.

She goes on: "I am sure there is some sense to be made of this, but I cannot make it" (200–201).

In the end, the Kesh are saved from the Condor by the Condor's own folly: determined to reinvent the war machines of the twentieth century, but lacking fossil fuels, they burn even their seed-corn to power a few ineffective airplanes called "Nestlings." (One remembers that the book was written in the years of Ronald Reagan's Star Wars project, and the massive deficit budgets that powered it.)

If the opposition of the Kesh and the Condor were all, the book would seem fairly simply didactic, a tract in favor of bioregionalism and against most of the baggage of Western culture. (Though its human drama would still reside in the mixed loyalties of Stone Telling and her Condor father, who is named "Kills" but in fact sacrifices his own life to get his daughter back to the Kesh.)

But it is not all; there is a third culture to be reckoned with. The computers have survived the cataclysm and created their own immortal, self-repairing network, spread over much of the universe and called "the City of Mind." (The word "City" is used elsewhere, by the Kesh, only in two contexts—for the past ages of "civilization" and for the urban centers of the Condor people.) The City's "existence consisted essentially in information"; its business is gathering data on all subjects whatsoever, from all parts of the known universe. The City neither interferes with nor tries to influence biological life, but it makes its knowledge available to human beings on request, through computer terminals, or "Exchanges," located in all sizeable communities. "[T]he goal of the Mind was to become a total mental model or replica of the Universe" (149–51).

The Kesh, and Le Guin, seem ambivalent whether to consider the City alive, or human. It does, after all, pursue "the business of any species or individual: to go on existing." It is even an example of "conscious, self-directed evolution" (149–50). The City "seems to recognize its ancient origins in human artifacts," referring to the human species as "makers." To the Kesh, however, they and the City are "two species [that] had diverged to the extent that competition between them was nonexistent, cooperation limited, and the question of superiority or inferiority bootless" (152).

It is an extraordinary fable, for what it implies, and makes seem almost necessary, is an evolutionary splitting-off of what I have called the "cosmopolitan impulse," what much of European thought considers the defining characteristic of humanity. It is not—and this is important—identical with the Condors' patriarchal principle, the desire to dominate. But neither is it entirely suited to biological embodiment. The Kesh, however useful they may find the Exchanges, are clear enough in excluding the City's goals from their sense of the proper purpose of life: "they were not disposed to regard human existence either as information or as communication, nor intelligent mortality as a means to the ends of immortal intelligence" (152).

This fable makes clear, I think, at once how strong the impulse is, in bioregionalism, to get rid of the Cartesian identification of human identity with disinterested thought; and how intractable that identification proves. It may split off into a fiber-metallic body, but it will not disappear. The same tension is preserved in the ending of the book. (I take the "ending" to be the ending of the narrative proper, excluding the encyclopedically organized "Back of the Book.") For the narrative does not conclude with Stone Telling's return and the disappearance of the Condor but with an earlier event, the expulsion of the Warrior Lodge from the Valley. The Warriors are a group of men who, while ostensibly preparing to defend the Valley from the Condors, have essentially accepted the Condor ideology. In the contentious meeting that leads to the expulsion, the Warriors are accused of having "fall[en] sick with the Sickness of Man," of being "a mouth on the back of a head talking" (382–83). To this, one of the Warriors, aptly named "Skull," replies: "You say that you fear our sickness. So it may be. Then I say this: our sickness is our humanity. To be human is to be sick. The lion is well, the hawk is well, the oak is well, they live and die in the mindfulness of the sacred, and need take no care. But from us sacredness has withdrawn care; in us is the mind of the sacred. So all we do is careful, all our effort is to be mindful, and yet we are not whole."

The Kesh, Skull contends, are creating an elaborate fiction when they name themselves for animals, plants, stones, and "deny that [they] are outcast" from the fellowship of nature. This denial, this "comfort-seeking," is itself the Original Sin for which they deserve punishment (384).

It is the old gnostic argument, that human beings can only be fictively at home in this world, being set apart by language and the nature of consciousness. It runs through both religious and antireligious strains in Western thought, from medieval Catholicism, to the Rilke *Elegy* I quoted earlier, to Derrida. In our own Far West tradition, it is the conclusion Yvor Winters came to in Madrid, New Mexico. Though the argument arouses great anger among the Kesh, it is never refuted; the few unregenerate Warriors simply slip away of their own accord. And, indeed, the anonymous narrator of the section ends by giving some credence to Skull's speech: "I have come to think that the sickness of Man is like the mutating viruses and the toxins: there will always be some form of it about. . . . What those sick with it said is true: It is a sickness of our being human, a fearful one" (386). And indeed, as indirect evidence, I find in my own experience of reading *Always Coming Home* that the stories that stay in my mind are those involving alienation, transgression, out-of-body and out-of-culture experiences: Stone Telling and her father, the "visionary" Flicker, the wildness of the Moon Dance. It is these contrasts that give the utopian image of centeredness its background glow.

As Yeats said, famously, rhetoric comes out of a quarrel with others, poetry out of a quarrel with oneself. The presence of these tensions in two major works from the two ends of the twentieth century tempts me to a generalization: that much of the poetry in western American literature comes from the fact that the impulse to inhabitation, passionate though it is, does not exist alone. Over against it stand both the strangeness and newness of the place itself, and the imagination of a richer knowledge or culture existing elsewhere, be it in Europe, Japan, or the "City of Mind." If we *are* always coming home, we are also, like Thea, always departing; and this double awareness gives western literature, I would argue, much of its special inflection. But I have to admit that this generalization serves my own wishes; it makes me feel, as a transplanted cosmopolitan, that the consciousness behind the literature of my chosen place is, in the deepest way, my own.

Epilogue

In a bad storm year, the whole south end of Carmel beach can disappear, as the high waves pound directly against the bluffs at the back. Then the underlying rocks—visible at no other time—emerge, partly or sometimes wholly, from under the vanishing sand. Sandstone chiefly, they have neither the age nor the solidity of the rocks in India that E. M. Forster called "flesh of the sun's flesh." Yet there is something curiously biological, something eternal and forgotten, about their forms. First one long, orange-tan ridge surfaces, a rounded back like a breaching whale. Its color and texture are fleshlike: gentle, tawny, granular-smooth. Then comes another, dark-purplish stratum, covered, it seems, with a forest of stone mushrooms, several inches wide, an inch or two apart. When it emerges fully, this ridge stands three or four feet tall, with little inlets and grottoes, like a coral reef, their floors still barely underwater at low tide. Small fish—and sometimes children—run in and out.

You can still walk for stretches, climbing over these various ridges, skirting the tide on precarious fringes of sand in between. You might find giant chitons, which you could mistake for abalone, until a seashore-life book, preserved from childhood, tells you differently—noting their brick-orange rubbery texture, with ridges of internal armor just traceable underneath, and the tiny cilia along the sides. You might find small rocks torn up and cast ashore with their seaweed still rooted to them. But later, if the storms are bad enough, all the sand disappears; by January the whole southern beach is unbroken water. Huge drift logs are tossed about like sticks in the coves.

Looking at these things, I sometimes feel I have been given back a kind of second sight, which is at once the asexual clarity of childhood and the eye that looks on Last Things. The thought forms in my mind, unbidden: *this is where we come to die.* Perhaps it's an accident of my family history. My mother lived out her nineties in a house two blocks inland, as my grandfather and grandmother did before her. My father's bones rest in El Carmelo cemetery, near Steinbeck's great tide pool, five miles away. He in fact chose to come West—made the first airplane flight of his life, five weeks before its end—so they could rest there.

Yet I find the thought has occurred to other western writers before me: that the West, the California coast in particular, is a place to die, a place to face ultimates. Jeffers is full of this sense of finality, of the coast as the "theater-stage" where "our blood . . . [will] play its mystery before strict judges at last."[1] Even William Everson's panegyric contains some dark sentences, after Everson is forced to agree with Kevin Starr about the "death-drift" in turn-of-the-century writers like Jack London and George Sterling, and its influence on the young Jeffers.

> West is the sundown quarter, and sundown means death.
> Long before the sun sets the gathering shadow hovers over
> the land, announcing the actual disappearance of the light.
> In California this haunting terminal darkness is mani-
> fested in many ways.

Partly it is a matter of geography and American myth, the sense of what Jeffers called "Continent's End." After the frontier, and its promise of illimitably renewed hope, "the abrupt sense of end-stop, the feeling of nowhere further to go, awakens a strong inertia in the life-energy." This "haunting terminal darkness," Everson suggests, may explain some of the qualities onlookers find disturbing in California life, and in California literature. These include a "masculine penchant for violence," but also a "disquieting lassitude in the California scene, which East Coast commentators have long dwelt on"—so that even Edmund Wilson proves partly right in the end, spiritually if not aesthetically. The "vast step beyond" the continent's end may be the "Far East," as Snyder and others would maintain, but it could also be the Lethelands of "[a]lcohol, sexual exigence, strange psychedelic hybrids.

. . . [I]t should not go unremarked that California's state flower is the poppy."[2]

Everson's piece of course addresses its own cultural moment: the bohemianism of the 1960s, like that of the 1900s, ended especially darkly here, with satanism, Manson, Altamont. Yet his idea of a "sundown" archetype finds echoes elsewhere. I have found it, for instance, in two particularly moving poems by late twentieth-century poets transplanted to California. Virginia Hamilton Adair's "Blackened Rings" begins by recalling the pioneer days, when moving westward literally

> was to cry farewell until death do us join
> to all the faces
> the little fences of the East.[3]

In her own day, the physical journey back is easy, "the slow wheels having grown wings." But the spiritual journey remains imponderably difficult:

> How should I turn again past death
> past life, go down the grainlands
> toward that narrower sea?
> finding the dreams have faces
> and the places fences
> and myself a mere hovering
> spun of some traveler's frosty breath

"[P]ast death / past life" is a strange phrase. On one level, I suppose it refers to all the poet has lived through since her transplantation; the great act of one's destiny pledges one to the place where it occurred, welcome or not. But on another level, surely the phrase suggests that the West itself is somehow a place "past death / past life": that the earlier country where hope (or the unconscious) seems more closely meshed with possibilities, where "dreams have faces," is now, like its ocean, "narrower" than the transhumanity that has been discovered. Adair cannot go back, finally, because she shares Everson's intuition:

> but my blood tells me that the trail ends here
> at the vast waters of the sleeping sun.

Does this mean that the East is the place of life? Slogging through the long winter in boots and heavy overcoats; the heart-breaking faintness of the first traces of green, under the prolonged gray skies; then the glory the moist air gives to summer . . . One would think that the annual metaphorical approach to death would make death seem nearer; in fact, the reverse may be true. Cycles reassure us that time is real, and that we are immersed in it, that our dreams, in Adair's haunting phrase, do "have faces." The relative absence, or subtlety, of cycles may make us feel that we are already outside of time. Or at least, so it can seem to the transplanted. Czeslaw Milosz captures this feeling in his poem "A Magic Mountain," a poem that gave me considerable wry comfort during my first disoriented years out here:

> I don't remember exactly when Budberg died, it was
> either two years ago or three.
> The same with Chen. Whether last year or the one before.[4]

Milosz remembers Budberg, a fellow Lithuanian, telling him that "in the beginning it is hard to get accustomed, / For here there is no spring or summer, no winter or fall," and adding

> "Where so little changes you hardly notice how time
> goes by.
> This is, you will see, a magic mountain."

The allusion to Mann's novel is, of course, a very bitter one. Is Berkeley *really* like the tuberculosis sanitarium, where the patients, some perhaps malingerers, all removed from what seems to them significant life, "get used to not getting used to it," and are taken utterly by surprise by the First World War? Milosz's sense that exile amounts to not-living is understandably acuter than most, given the historic grandeur, and the cataclysms, of the world he comes from. "So I won't have power, won't save the world?"

> Did I then train myself, myself the Unique,
> To compose stanzas for gulls and sea haze,
> To listen to the foghorns blaring down below?

But, of course, this is not merely the exile's complaint. It is the universal complaint of the human ego, for whom no conditions, no surroundings, are quite propitious enough. "The Earth has not been to Your Majesty's liking," Milosz says to that ego, in another poem from around the same time as "A Magic Mountain," "The Separate Notebooks."

And it is on this level that the problem must be addressed. Elsewhere in "The Separate Notebooks," Milosz sees the West even more grimly, as uncreated, or a kind of pre-creation, as Father Latour saw New Mexico in Cather:

> The earth in its nakedness of hard lava carved by river
>   beds, the vast
> earth, void, before the vegetation.
>
> And the river they came to, called by adventurers Colum-
>   bia, rolls down
> her waters, a cold and liquid lava as gray as if there were
>   neither sky
> nor white clouds above.

"The spirit of the place," in California, is "Hills the color of straw, and the rocks assembled / Like Jurassic reptiles." Yet this is the point: to inhabit such a place is to recognize what our visions of home conceal from us, the uncreatedness of life itself. Returning to "A Magic Mountain":

> One murky island with its barking seals
> Or a parched desert is enough
> To make us say: yes, *oui, si.*
> "Even asleep we partake in the becoming of the world."

So "defeat" becomes indistinguishable from triumph:

> With a flick of the wrist I fashioned an invisible rope
> And climbed it and it held me.

It is the exile's discovery, but it is also the human creative discovery. Really, in all of our projects, we are climbing on an idea into the always unknowable future.

Still, nothing quite prepares the reader for the apocalyptic celebration with which Milosz's poem ends. It is part academic procession, part the Dance of Death, on a hill as Ingmar Bergman envisioned it in *The Seventh Seal:*

What caps and hooded gowns!
Most respected Professor Budberg,
Most distinguished Professor Chen,
Wrong Honorable Professor Milosz,
Who wrote poems in some unheard-of tongue.
Who will count them anyway. And here sunlight,
So that the flames of their tall candles fade.

What is celebrated here, as the professors become one with, but as indistinguishable as, the "generations of hummingbirds," is something like Buddhist impermanence, whose meanings can be oddly positive as well as negative. There is a joy in completing, losing—and yet somehow redeeming—all the "Wrong" identities and ambitions as the small lights "fade" into the Light. And that Light continues to have an eerie yet humorous connection to the western seasonlessness:

And the fog from the ocean is cool, for once again it is
July.

I too have my light that stands for the final, all-absorbing Light, though it is different from Milosz's. It is the winter solstice light on Carmel Beach. I suppose preconscious memory must explain why it seems so utterly fresh to me, and yet to come both before and after sexuality and striving. It is so clarifying, though it comes from so low in the sky; so dry, though it falls between storms; a source neither of heat nor cold. It is, as T. S. Eliot wrote of a different "midwinter spring," "not in time's covenant."

And I too have felt stretched across landscapes, belonging to too many, until, like Virginia Hamilton Adair, I seemed "a mere hovering / spun of some traveler's frosty breath." The question of where I will die, mysterious for everyone, is perhaps a shade acuter for me. It might be in Greve in Chianti; it might be in the Himalayas, if I ever undertake that perilous journey. It might, by some miracle, be in the lushness of eastern summer. But there's a fair chance it will be here, in the house my grandparents built, two blocks from the bluffs and that last ocean. If so, it will seem fitting. My blood, too, "tells me that the trail ends here / at the vast waters of the sleeping sun."

Notes

PROLOGUE

1. Frank Bidart, "California Plush," in *In the Western Night: Collected Poems 1965–90* (New York: Farrar, Straus, and Giroux, 1990), 136.
2. Carol Muske-Dukes, "Slouching toward a Brief Literary History of Southern California," in *Married to the Icepick Killer* (New York: Random House, 2002), 34.
3. Edmund Wilson, "The Boys in the Back Room," in *Classics and Commercials* (New York: Farrar, Straus, and Co., 1950), 45–47.
4. Ibid., 45, 49.
5. William Everson, *Archetype West: The Pacific Coast as a Literary Region* (Berkeley: Oyez, 1976), 15, 5. Hereafter cited parenthetically in the text.
6. Wilson, "The Boys," 45–47.
7. Kevin Starr, *Americans and the California Dream* (New York and Oxford: Oxford University Press, 1973), 285–86.
8. Starr, *Americans,* 223ff.
9. Joel Porte, *The Romance in America* (Middletown, Conn.: Wesleyan University Press, 1969), 7.
10. William Carlos Williams, *In the American Grain* (New York: New Directions, 1956), 232, 228, 226.
11. Nathaniel Hawthorne, preface to *The Marble Faun* (New York: Dell, 1960), 23; Henry James, *Hawthorne* (New York: Harper and Brothers, 1879), 43.
12. Randall Jarrell, introduction to *The Selected Poems of William Carlos Williams* (New York: New Directions, 1963), xiv.
13. John Updike, *Rabbit Is Rich* (New York: Alfred A. Knopf, 1981), 379.
14. Muske-Dukes, *Married to the Icepick Killer,* 31.
15. Quoted in Erika Ostrovsky, *Under the Sign of Ambiguity: Saint-John Perse/Alexis Leger* (New York: New York University Press, 1985), 60; my translation.

CATHER AND ROMANCE

1. Willa Cather, *O Pioneers!* (Boston and New York: Houghton Mifflin Mariner Books, 1995), 3–4.

2. Willa Cather, *The Song of the Lark* (New York: Bantam Classics, 1991), 3–5, 8.

3. Willa Cather, *Death Comes for the Archbishop* (New York: Vintage, 1971), 17–18. Hereafter cited parenthetically in the text.

4. From the openings, respectively, of *The Pathfinder, The House of the Seven Gables, The Marble Faun.*

5. Richard Chase, *The American Novel and Its Tradition* (Garden City: Doubleday Anchor Books, 1957), xi.

6. Ibid., 12–13.

7. Ibid., 14.

8. Hawthorne, *The Marble Faun,* 23.

9. Chase, *The American Novel,* 13.

10. Willa Cather, "On *Death Comes for the Archbishop,*" in *Willa Cather on Writing* (New York: Alfred A. Knopf, 1949), 9.

11. "The Novel Demeublé," in *Willa Cather on Writing* (New York: Alfred A. Knopf, 1949), 41.

12. Chase, *The American Novel,* 7.

13. Quoted in James Woodress, *Willa Cather: A Literary Life* (Lincoln and London: University of Nebraska Press: 1987), 36.

14. Cather quoted in Sharon O'Brien, *Willa Cather: The Emerging Voice* (New York and Oxford: Oxford University Press, 1987), 64.

15. Cather, "The Novel Demeublé," 51.

YOSEMITE PAINTERS

1. David Robertson, *West of Eden: A History of the Art and Literature of Yosemite* (Yosemite: Yosemite Natural History Association and Wilderness Press, 1984), 21.

2. Ibid., 45.

3. Ibid., 23–26.

4. Ibid., 27–28.

5. Ibid., 30–31.

6. Jorie Graham, "Pollock and Canvas," in *The End of Beauty* (New York: Ecco Press, 1987), 84.

7. John Muir, *The Yosemite* (New York: Appleton-Century, 1912), 99.

8. Quoted in Starr, *Americans and the California Dream,* 422.

TWO CONVALESCENTS

1. D. H. Lawrence, *St. Mawr* (New York: Vintage Books, 1960), 140. Hereafter cited parenthetically in the text.

2. D. H. Lawrence, "New Mexico," in Keith Sagar, *D. H. Lawrence and New Mexico,* ed. Keith Sagar (Salt Lake City: Peregrine Smith, 1982), 96. Hereafter cited parenthetically in the text.

3. D. H. Lawrence, *Sons and Lovers* (Cambridge and New York: Cambridge University Press, 1992), 291.

4. *The Letters of D. H. Lawrence*, ed. Aldous Huxley (London: Heinemann, 1932), 542–46.

5. D. H. Lawrence, *Women in Love* (New York: Modern Library, 1950), 195; letter quoted in Paul Delany, *D. H. Lawrence's Nightmare* (Basic Books: New York, 1978), 84.

6. D. H. Lawrence, "The Hopi Snake Dance," in *D. H. Lawrence and New Mexico*, ed. Keith Sagar (Salt Lake City: Peregrine Smith, 1982), 66. Hereafter cited parenthetically in the text.

7. Christopher Sindt, "The Poetics of Biophilia: Natural Object-Relations in Lawrence, Roethke, and Plath" (PhD diss., University of California, Davis, 2000), 138, 148. Marianna Torgovnick, in *Primitive Passions* (New York: Alfred A. Knopf, 1997), also views Lawrence's affinity for Native American religion sympathetically, though arguing, oversimply I think, that if it had not been for his Western resistances he would have identified entirely with the principle of cosmic oneness.

8. See Sagar, *D. H. Lawrence in New Mexico*, 14–17.

9. D. H. Lawrence, "Reflections on the Death of a Porcupine," in *D. H. Lawrence and New Mexico*, ed. Keith Sagar (Salt Lake City: Peregrine Smith, 1982), 88. Hereafter cited parenthetically in the text.

10. See Lawrence, *Women in Love*, 196.

11. D. H. Lawrence, *Fantasia of the Unconscious and Psychoanalysis and the Unconscious* (New York and London: Penguin, 1971), 98. Hereafter cited parenthetically in the text.

12. See Alan Williamson, *Almost a Girl: Male Writers and Female Identification* (Charlottesville: University Press of Virginia, 2001), chap. 3.

13. Introduction to *The Early Poems of Yvor Winters* (Denver: Alan Swallow, 1966), 11. All subsequent quotations of Winters's poetry are taken from this volume.

14. Terry Comito, *In Defense of Winters* (Madison: University of Wisconsin Press, 1986), 102.

15. Yvor Winters, *In Defense of Reason* (New York: Swallow Press and William Morrow, 1947), 593.

16. "The Dance," in *The Complete Poems and Selected Letters of Hart Crane* (New York: Doubleday Anchor, 1966), 70–72. I take the term "intersubjectivity," advisedly, from Jessica Benjamin, and from Christopher Sindt's application of the ideas of Harold Searles, in the dissertation cited in note 7 above.

17. Robert Hass, "Yvor Winters / What He Did," in *Twentieth Century Pleasures* (Hopewell, N.J.: Ecco Press, 1984), 145–46.

18. Thomas Parkinson, *Hart Crane and Yvor Winters: Their Literary Correspondence* (Berkeley and Los Angeles: University of California Press, 1978), 133.

LAS TRAMPAS, CHIMAYO, THE GEORGIA O'KEEFFE MUSEUM

1. Some of the information here comes from Alice Bullock, *Mountain Villages* (Santa Fe: Sunstone Press, 1981); and Elizabeth Kay, *Chimayo Valley Traditions* (Santa Fe: Ancient City Press, 1987). Most comes from my own notes, taken in July 1998.

2. Mark Stevens, "Introduction: Georgia O'Keeffe and the American Dream," *The Georgia O'Keeffe Museum*, edited by Peter H. Hassrick (New York: Harry N. Abrams, 1997), 16.

3. Barbara Rose, "O'Keeffe's Originality," in *The Georgia O'Keeffe Museum (New York: Harry N. Abrams, 1997)*, 100.

4. Stevens, "Introduction: Georgia O'Keeffe and the American Dream," 15.

TAMAR AND TONALISM

1. Harvey L. Jones, *Twilight and Reverie: California Tonalist Painting, 1890–1930* (Oakland Museum, 1995), 2.

2. Ibid., 5.

3. Robinson Jeffers and Horace Lyon, *Jeffers Country* (San Francisco: Scrimshaw Press, 1971), 10.

4. Robinson Jeffers, "Thurso's Landing," in *The Selected Poetry of Robinson Jeffers* (New York: Random House, 1937), 268. All subsequent quotations of Jeffers's poetry are from this edition, except where noted.

5. Robinson Jeffers, *Cawdor*, in *"Cawdor" and "Medea"* (New York: New Directions, 1970), 19.

6. In conversation.

7. Robert Zaller, in *The Cliffs of Solitude* (Cambridge and New York: Cambridge University Press, 1983), 16–23, makes a good case for the ontological significance of Tamar's actions, drawing on John T. Irwin's readings of Faulkner in *Doubling and Incest*. Still, I suspect, for most readers who manage to finish the poem, the primary impression is their sensationalism.

8. Jeffers, *Cawdor*, 29.

9. Robert Hass, introduction to *Rock and Hawk: A Selection of Shorter Poems by Robinson Jeffers*, ed. Hass (New York: Random House, 1987), xxxii.

10. *Carmel Pine Cone*, June 29, 1922; reprinted in *Californians*.

11. See Karl F. Zender, "Faulkner and the Politics of Incest," *American Literature* 70 (1998): 739–65.

12. Robinson Jeffers, *Roan Stallion*, in *Rock and Hawk: A Selection of Shorter Poems by Robinson Jeffers*, ed. Robert Hass (New York: Random House, 1987).

13. Robinson Jeffers, *Medea*, in *"Cawdor" and "Medea"* (New York: New Directions, 1970), 114, 142.

THE PERSISTENCE OF JEFFERS

1. Randall Jarrell, *The Third Book of Criticism* (New York: Farrar, Straus, and Giroux, 1969), 322.

2. Robinson Jeffers, *The Selected Poetry of Robinson Jeffers* (New York: Random House, 1937). All subsequent quotations of Jeffers's poetry are from this edition, except where noted.

3. Jonathan Edwards, "Sinners in the Hands of an Angry God," in *Selections*, ed. Clarence H. Faust and Thomas H. Johnson (New York: Hill and Wang, 1962), 164.

4. Sandra McPherson, "Fringecups," in *Streamers* (New York: Ecco Press, 1988), 66; Brenda Hillman, "Canyon," in *Fortress* (Middletown, Conn.: Wesleyan University Press, 1989), 59–60.

5. William Wordsworth, *The Prelude*, book 1, ll. 393–400.

6. Philip Hobsbaum, *Metre, Rhythm, and Verse Form* (London and New York: Routledge, 1996), 105.

7. Robert Hass, *Rock and Hawk: A Selection of Shorter Poems by Robinson Jeffers* (New York: Random House, 1987), 227, 232.

8. Robinson Jeffers, "Contemplation of the Sword," in *Rock and Hawk* (New York: Random House, 1987).

STEINBECK, SCIENCE, AND THE TAO

1. Susan Shillinglaw, "Introduction: A Steinbeck Scholar's Perspective," in *Steinbeck and the Environment*, ed. Susan F. Beegel, Susan Shillinglaw, and Wesley N. Tiffney Jr. (Tuscaloosa and London: University of Alabama Press, 1997), 11.

2. John Steinbeck, *Cannery Row* (New York: Bantam, 1954), 17–18. Hereafter cited parenthetically in the text.

3. A. R. Ammons, "Corson's Inlet," in *Selected Poems* (Ithaca, N.Y.: Cornell University Press, 1968), 139.

4. See, particularly, Peter Lisca, *John Steinbeck: Nature and Myth* (New York: Cromwell, 1978), 116–20.

5. *Tao Te Ching*, trans. Stephen Mitchell (New York: HarperPerennial, 1988), 64, 57.

6. Wilson, "The Boys in the Back Room," 38–39.

7. Yano Shigeharu, preface to *John Steinbeck: Asian Perspectives*, ed. Kiyoshi Nakayama, Scott Pugh, and Shigeharu Yano (Osaka: Osaka Kyoiku Tosho, 1992).

8. Susan F. Beegel, "Introduction: A Generalist's Perspective," in *Steinbeck and the Environment*, ed. Susan F. Beegel, Susan Shillinglaw, and Wesley N. Tiffney Jr. (Tuscaloosa and London: University of Alabama Press, 1997), 14–15.

9. John Steinbeck, *The Log from the Sea of Cortez* (New York and London: Penguin, 1977), 146. Hereafter cited parenthetically in the text.

10. Louis Owens, "An Essay in Loneliness," in *John Steinbeck's Re-vision of*

America (Athens: University of Georgia Press, 1985), 180–90. See also Kiyohiko Tsuboi, "*Cannery Row* Reconsidered," in *Asian Perspectives,* ed. Kiyoshi Nakayama, Scott Pugh, and Shigeharu Yano (Osaka: Osaka Kyoiku Tosho, 1992), esp. 117–18.

11. *The Gateless Barrier,* trans. Robert Aitken (San Francisco: North Point, 1990), 7.

12. For more on the importance of this phrase to Steinbeck, see James C. Kelley, "John Steinbeck and Ed Ricketts: Understanding Life in the Great Tidepool," in *Steinbeck and the Environment,* ed. Susan F. Beegel, Susan Shillinglaw, and Wesley N. Tiffney Jr. (Tuscaloosa and London: University of Alabama Press, 1997), esp. 30–31.

13. Louis Owens, *John Steinbeck's Re-vision of America* (Athens: University of Georgia Press, 1985), 189.

"TOO MUCH WHAT THEY'D THOUGHT"

1. James McMichael, *Four Good Things* (Boston: Houghton Mifflin, 1980), 43. Hereafter cited parenthetically in the text.

2. Alan Williamson, *Introspection and Contemporary Poetry* (Cambridge: Harvard University Press, 1984), 178.

3. Raymond Chandler, *Farewell, My Lovely* (New York: Vintage Crime, 1992), 57, 42.

4. Elliot L. Gilbert, *The World of Mystery Fiction: A Guide* (San Diego: University Extension, University of California, San Diego, 1978), 7.

5. Raymond Chandler, *The Long Goodbye* (New York: Vintage Crime, 1992), 23. Hereafter cited parenthetically in the text.

6. Raymond Chandler, *The Little Sister,* in *Later Novels and Other Writings* (New York: Library of America, 1995), 414. Hereafter cited parenthetically in the text.

7. For a general discussion of this plot, see Northrop Frye, *The Anatomy of Criticism* (Princeton: Princeton University Press, 1957), 163–71.

8. Ibid., 179, 192.

9. Ibid., 171, 179.

10. There is also, perhaps, a psychoanalytic explanation for this distrust of desire, in the absence of authority. As Jessica Benjamin argues in *The Bonds of Love* (New York: Pantheon, 1988), children whose parents oppose no resistance to their desires are not in fact freer. They feel "emptiness and loss of connection" and may even fear they have destroyed their parents by the strength of their desires; hence they can be extremely punitive to their own impulses in fantasy, while at the same time outwardly insisting on having their own way (35; see also 39).

11. For a somewhat different psychoanalytic explanation of why the plot with an absent or corrupt father requires a femme fatale, see Slavoj Žižek, "Why Are There Always Two *Fathers*?" in *Enjoy Your Symptom* (New York and London: Routledge, 2001).

12. Benjamin, *Bonds of Love,* 164.

13. Gilbert, *The World of Mystery Fiction*, 106.

14. See Russell Davies, "Omnes Me Impune Lacessunt," in *The World of Raymond Chandler*, ed. Miriam Gross (London: Weidenfeld and Nicolson, 1977), 31–42.

15. See Michael Mason, "Marlowe, Men, and Women," in *The World of Raymond Chandler*, ed. Miriam Gross (London: Weidenfeld and Nicolson, 1977), 89–101; and Gershon Legman, *Love and Death: A Study in Censorship* (New York: Breaking Point, 1949).

16. Mason, "Marlowe, Men, and Women," 98–99.

17. Elizabeth Ward and Alain Silver, *Raymond Chandler's Los Angeles* (Woodstock, N.Y.: Overlook Press, 1987), 13.

18. J. O. Tate, "The Longest Goodbye: Raymond Chandler and the Poetry of Alcohol," *Armchair Detective* 18 (fall 1985): 393.

19. Natasha Spender, "His Own Long Goodbye," in *The World of Raymond Chandler*, ed. Miriam Gross (London: Weidenfeld and Nicolson, 1977), 149.

20. Spender, "His Own Long Goodbye," 134–35.

21. Frank Bidart, "California Plush," in *In the Western Night: Collected Poems 1965–1990* (New York: Farrar, Straus, and Giroux, 1990), 135. All subsequent quotations of Bidart's poetry are from *In the Western Night*.

22. Nicholas O. Warner, "City of Illusion: The Role of Hollywood in California Detective Fiction," *Armchair Detective* 16, no. 1 (1983): 24.

HIGHWAY 66

1. *VIA* (May/June 2001): 4, 42–51.

2. Gail Levin, *Edward Hopper: The Art and the Artist* (New York: W. W. Norton in association with the Whitney Museum, 1980), 49–50.

3. Leslie Marmon Silko, *Ceremony* (New York and London: Penguin, 1986), 116, 107. Hereafter cited parenthetically in the text.

4. Any term for native peoples, in the hands of a Euro-American writer, is potentially problematic. I use the word "Indian" because it is Silko's word.

5. Leslie Marmon Silko, "Interior and Exterior Landscapes," in *Yellow Woman and a Beauty of the Spirit* (New York: Simon and Schuster, 1996), 33.

6. David Abram, *The Spell of the Sensuous* (New York: Vintage, 1996), 176–77.

7. See Edith Swan, "Laguna Symbolic Geography and Silko's *Ceremony*," *American Indian Quarterly* 12 (1988): 244.

8. Louis Owens, *Other Destinies* (Norman and London: University of Oklahoma Press, 1992), 187. For a different application of the story, in which Tayo's role is more that of Yellow Woman, Ts'eh's of the Ka't'sina, see Elizabeth Hoffman Nelson and Malcolm A. Nelson, "Shifting Patterns, Changing Stories: Leslie Marmon Silko's Yellow Women," in *Leslie Marmon Silko: A Collection of Critical Essays*, ed. Louise K.

Barnett and James L. Thorson, 121–33 (Albuquerque: University of New Mexico Press, 1999).

9. Abram, *Spell of the Sensuous*, 178; emphasis in original.

10. Owens, *Other Destinies*, 3.

11. Ibid., 169.

12. T. S. Eliot, Notes to *The Waste Land*, in *The Complete Poems and Plays* (New York: Harcourt Brace, 1952), 52. The connection with Eliot has been noted, not favorably, by Shamoon Zamir, in "Literature in a 'National Sacrifice Area': Leslie Silko's *Ceremony*," in *New Voices in Native American Literary Criticism*, ed. Arnold Krupat, 396–415 (Washington and London: Smithsonian Institution Press, 1993).

13. Paula Gunn Allen, "Special Problems in Teaching Leslie Marmon Silko's *Ceremony*," *American Indian Quarterly* 14 (1990): 383.

14. Jana Sequoya, "How(!) Is an Indian," in *New Voices in Native American Literary Criticism* (Washington and London: Smithsonian Institution Press, 1993), 468.

THIEBAUD AND THE CITY

1. Karen Tsujimoto, *Wayne Thiebaud* (Seattle and London: University of Washington Press, 1985), plate 65.

2. Ibid., 43.

3. Ibid., 130–31.

SOME TENSES OF SNYDER

1. Gary Snyder, "A Walk," in *The Back Country* (New York: New Directions, 1968), 19.

2. Shunryu Suzuki, *Zen Mind, Beginner's Mind* (Weatherhill: New York and Tokyo, 1973), 30. Hereafter cited parenthetically in the text.

3. Gary Snyder, "Bubbs Creek Haircut," in *Mountains and Rivers Without End* (Washington, D.C.: Counterpoint, 1996), 36.

4. Wallace Stevens, "The American Sublime," in *The Palm at the End of the Mind* (New York: Vintage, 1972), 114.

5. Lawrence, *St. Mawr*, 152–53.

CHINA TRADE (I)

1. Gary Snyder, "Poetry and the Primitive," in *Look Out: A Selection of Writings* (New York: New Directions, 2002), 115.

2. Stephen Owen, *Traditional Chinese Poetry and Poetics: Omen of the World* (Madison: University of Wisconsin Press, 1985), 226.

3. T'ao Yuan-Ming, "Poem without a Category, No. 7," in *The Columbia Book of Chinese Poetry*, ed. Burton Watson (New York: Columbia University Press, 1984), 137; Su Tung-p'o, "Rhyming with Tzu-yu's 'At Mien-ch'ih, Recalling the Past," in *Selected Poems of Su Tung-p'o*, trans. Burton Watson (Port Townsend: Copper Canyon, 1994), 22.

4. Rainer Maria Rilke, "Buddha," in *New Poems [1907]*, trans. Edward Snow (San Francisco: North Point, 1984), 49.

5. Gary Snyder, "Hay for the Horses," in *No Nature: New and Selected Poems* (New York: Pantheon, 1992), 11.

6. Gary Snyder, *Mountains and Rivers without End* (Washington, D.C.: Counterpoint, 1996), 5. All subsequent quotations of Snyder's poetry are from this work.

7. See, in particular, Eric Todd Smith, *Reading Gary Snyder's "Mountains and Rivers Without End"* (Boise: Boise State University Press, 2000); and Rod Romesburg, "Butterfly in the Garden: Chaos, Order, and Contemporary Nature Writing," PhD diss., University of California at Davis, 1999.

8. Gary Snyder, "Piute Creek," in *No Nature: New and Selected Poems* (New York: Pantheon, 1992), 6.

9. Program notes, *Mountains and Rivers Without End*, read in its entirety by Gary Snyder, August 11, 2000. My student Charles Carlise has done an illuminating study of just how minutely Snyder's text parallels the Japanese original.

ARISTOTLE IN MONTANA

1. *Aristotle's Poetics*, trans. S. H. Butcher, with an introductory essay by Francis Ferguson (New York: Hill and Wang, 1984), 77.

2. Norman Maclean, "Episode, Scene, Speech, and Word: The Madness of Lear," in *Critics and Criticism* (abridged edition), ed. R. S. Crane (Chicago and London: University of Chicago Press, 1957), 101. Hereafter cited parenthetically in the text.

3. Norman Maclean, *Young Men and Fire* (Chicago and London: University of Chicago Press, 1992), 28. Hereafter cited parenthetically in the text.

4. The Custer parallel is quite prominent for a few pages. But even though Custer too died against his expectations, overwhelmed with western otherness, "red terror clos[ing] in from behind and above and from the sides" (146), Maclean seems to sense that he is too morally problematic a parallel to serve for long. References to him disappear at about the point where the Christian ones become especially prominent.

5. "For, to speak of an artistic attainment as possessing magnitude in the highest degree is to imply the existence of attainments somewhat analogous and in this or that respect somewhat inferior" ("Lear," 95).

6. See Marie Borroff, "The Achievement of Norman Maclean," *Yale Review* 82, no. 2 (April 1994), esp. 121–22.

7. Richard Wertime, letter to author.

8. *Aristotle's Poetics*, 61, 35.

9. Francis Ferguson, in his introductory essay to *Aristotle's Poetics* (New York: Hill and Wang, 1984), writes that "Having given us fear enough, they [the 'masters of tragedy'] melt us with pity . . . reconciling us to our fate, because we understand it as the universal human lot" (35), and that, at the end of tragedy, "passion, or pathos, takes over" (23).

10. George Steiner, *The Death of Tragedy* (New York: Oxford University Press, 1980), 8–9, 13. I am deeply grateful to my friend Scott MacLean (no relation to Norman), for steering me to these quotations.

CHINA TRADE (11)

1. Peter Dale Scott, *Listening to the Candle* (New York: New Directions, 1992).
2. Jane Hirschfield, "In Praise of Coldness," in *Given Sugar, Given Salt* (New York: Harper Collins, 2001). All subsequent quotations of Hirschfield's poems are from this volume.
3. Brenda Hillman, "Meridian Plinth," in *Bright Existence* (Hanover and London: Wesleyan University Press, 1993), 49–50.
4. Brenda Hillman, "Broken Dreams," in *Fortress* (Middletown, Conn.: Wesleyan University Press, 1989), 14.
5. "A Foghorn," in *Bright Existence* (Hanover and London: Wesleyan University Press, 1993), 68–69. All subsequent quotations of Hillman's poems are from this volume.
6. Robert Hass, "Images," in *Twentieth-Century Pleasures* (New York: Ecco Press, 1984), 270.
7. Robert Hass, "My Mother's Nipples," in *Sun Under Wood* (New York: Ecco Press, 1996). All subsequent quotations of Hass's work are from this poem.
8. Frank Bidart, "Book of Life," in *In the Western Night*, 144.

ALWAYS COMING HOME

1. Jacob Burckhardt, *The Civilization of the Renaissance in Italy* (London: Allen and Unwin, 1944), 83–84.
2. Willa Cather, *The Song of the Lark* (New York: Bantam Classics, 1991), 112. Hereafter cited parenthetically in the text.
3. Robert Pinsky, *An Explanation of America* (Princeton: Princeton University Press, 1979), 18–19.
4. *Tao Te Ching*, trans. Stephen Mitchell (New York: HarperPerennial, 1991), chap. 80.
5. Rilke, *Sonnets to Orpheus*, I, III (my renderings).
6. Gary Snyder, *"Riprap" and "Cold Mountain Poems"* (San Francisco: North Point, 1990), 61.
7. Le Guin's remarks are quoted, to the best of my memory, from a question-and-answer session at the University of California, Davis, April 1991.
8. Ursula K. Le Guin, *Always Coming Home* (Berkeley and Los Angeles: University of California Press, 2001), 153. Hereafter cited parenthetically in the text.
9. Rainer Maria Rilke, "The Eighth Elegy," in *The Selected Poetry of Rainer Maria Rilke*, trans. Stephen Mitchell (New York: Vintage, 1982), 192–93.

EPILOGUE

1. Robinson Jeffers, *Selected Poems*, 357.
2. Everson, *Archetype West*, 60–61.
3. Virginia Hamilton Adair, "Blackened Rings," in *Ants on the Melon* (New York: Random House, 1996), 50–51.
4. Czeslaw Milosz, "A Magic Mountain," in *The Collected Poems* (New York: Ecco Press, 1988). All subsequent quotations of Milosz's poetry are from *The Collected Poems*.

Index